Social Service Reform in the Postcommunist State

Eugenia and Hugh M. Stewart '26
Series on Eastern Europe .
Stjepan Meštrović, General Editor

Social Service Reform in the Postcommunist State

Decentralization in Poland

Janelle A. Kerlin

Texas A&M University Press, College Station

First edition

The paper used in this book meets the minimum requirements
of the American National Standard for Permanence
of Paper for Printed Library Materials, Z39.48-1984.
Binding materials have been chosen for durability.
♾

Library of Congress Cataloging-in-Publication Data
Kerlin, Janelle A., 1969–
Social service reform in the postcommunist state : decentralization in Poland / Janelle A. Kerlin
p. cm. — (Eugenia and Hugh M. Stewart '26 series on Eastern Europe)
Includes bibliographical references and index.
ISBN 1-58544-417-0 (cloth : alk. paper)
1. Poland—Social policy. 2. Human services—Poland. 3. Decentralization in government—Poland. I. Title. II. Series.
HN537.5.K47 2005
361.6'1'09438—dc22

2004025469

For my grandmother, Arlene Kerlin

Contents

Illustrations

FIGURES

MAPS

Acknowledgments

I am grateful to many individuals and institutions in the United States and Poland for their help in the completion of this study. My greatest appreciation goes to Mitchell Orenstein, my dissertation advisor at the Maxwell School, Syracuse University, who provided expert guidance, support, and encouragement through the entire research and publication process. Many thanks also go to the dissertation committee for their helpful comments and suggestions, especially in preparation for publication: Suzanne Mettler, Larry Schroeder, Jeremy Shiffman, Richard Braungart from the Maxwell School, and Joanna Regulska from Rutgers University.

I also owe much to the invaluable assistance of many individuals in Poland. Ewa Leś, professor at the University of Warsaw, acted as in-field dissertation advisor and provided unfailing support and direction during my research stay in Warsaw. Those who were instrumental in the development of the survey include Jarosław Anisiewicz of the Włodawa town council, Przemysław Kasza of Pracownia Badań Społecznych (a survey research institute), Tomasz Kaźmierczak of the Institute for the Development of Social Services, Wojciech Marchlewski of the Association of Rural Municipalities, Sławomir Nałęcz of the Institute of Political Studies, Polish Academy of Sciences, Victor Wekselberg of the Local Government Partnership Program, Marek Wójcik of the Association of Polish Counties, and Krystyna Wyrwicka, director of the Department of Social Welfare, Polish Ministry of Labor and Social Policy. Special thanks also go to the many other politicians and government officials I interviewed and to Tony Levitas for going the extra mile in providing assistance in understanding the politics behind the reform.

I also gratefully acknowledge the financial and other material support I received that made this research possible. Financial support for the dissertation was provided by a Fulbright-Hays Dissertation Research Abroad Fellowship, an American Council of Learned Societies East European Dissertation Fellowship, and a Maxwell

Dean's Dissertation Fellowship. I also had the opportunity to complete the dissertation and initial revisions as a visiting dissertation fellow in the International Activities Center at the Urban Institute in Washington, D.C. Final revisions to the manuscript were made while I was an East European Studies Research Scholar at the Woodrow Wilson International Center for Scholars. Special thanks go to Tony Levitas, Włodzimierz Puzyna, Harry Hatry, Elizabeth Reid, and Conor O'Dwyer for reviewing parts of the text, to Jackie Jackson who pulled the maps together, and to Debbie Chin who helped with editing. Finally, this book would not have been possible without the many family and friends who provided ongoing support through the entire research and publication process.

Social Service Reform
in the Postcommunist State

1 Introduction

The fall of communism in East Central Europe opened the door for new governments to extend authority and decision-making power to citizens in lower-level government. Though much of the purpose of this first wave of decentralization was to undermine communist strongholds in heavily centralized bureaucracies, it was also relatively successful in bringing democracy and improved public services to lower levels of government. Later decentralization reforms increasingly focused on these theorized benefits of bringing government closer to the people. Such reforms, however, were undertaken in an entirely different political context—rather than early transitioning democracy, second round reforms were pursued in a context of consolidating democracy and increased international influence. In the case of Poland, this new context had significant implications not only for the political process of reform development but for reform outcomes as well. Indeed, the politics of decentralization often compromised reform goals and led to unintended consequences.

Poland's second round of decentralization, the 1999 public administration reform, was an immense undertaking that included administrative, political, and fiscal decentralization as well as territorial redivision of the state. It reduced the number of provinces from forty-nine to sixteen, restored the county level in the form of 373 counties (including sixty-five cities with county status), and decentralized central tasks and authority to these two levels. Broad goals focused formally on increased citizen involvement and improved public services though still informally on the further decommunization of the public bureaucracy.

Initial outcomes, however, show that the reform resulted in many unmet goals and unintended consequences. Democratization was only minimally increased as the central government retained both revenue-generating and revenue-assignment authority over most decentralized functions, which severely limited county and provincial self-government autonomy. Moreover, a number of functions intended for decentralization remained centralized, limiting

Map 1. Provincial division of Poland as of January 1, 1999 (sixteen provinces). Source: Jerzy Regulski, *Samorząd III Rzeczypospolitej.*

the scope of new subnational governments. Though decentralization improved some services by bringing them closer to recipients, poor funding did little to improve services in other ways and in some cases made them worse. Unintended consequences of the reform also included policies that worked at cross purposes, which resulted in such outcomes as increased disparity in services across urban and rural areas. In addition, the reform had mixed results particular to specific policy sectors, as a detailed examination of the reform in the area of social services reveals.

In this study I show that the politics of reform development involved tensions between competing interests within and outside the ruling coalition government, resulting in compromise and manipulation that led to less-than-satisfactory outcomes. I draw and build upon Schickler's concept of "disjointed pluralism" to explain this political process and resulting outcomes.[1] Disjointed pluralism is the idea that 1) many different formal and informal coalitions promoting a range of collective interests drive choices made in legislatures, and 2) the dynamics of reform development "derive from the *interactions* and *tensions* among competing formal and informal coalitions promoting several different interests."[2] Here the interactions and tensions that characterize the relationship between multiple interests drive processes of change that are ultimately reflected in legislative outcomes. As Schickler states, "conflicts among competing interests generate institutions that are rarely optimally tailored to meet any specific goal. As they adopt changes based on untidy compromises among multiple interests, members build institutions that are full of tensions and contradictions."[3] Though Schickler develops the concept of disjointed pluralism based on an analysis of the development of legislative institutions in the United States, its basic premises can be applied to the development of other public institutions in different democratic contexts, as this study on the politics of public administration reform in Poland demonstrates.[4]

While helping to explain much of the political compromise found with the reform, the theory of disjointed pluralism does not account for the influence of Poland's different political structure and some politics associated with neoliberal reformers in transitioning countries.[5] The presidential-parliamentary system found in Poland structures the political process in different ways than the presidential system in the United States—the system Schickler bases his analysis on. This study considers how Poland's different political framework structures the political behavior identified in Schickler's work through an examination of veto points in the Polish system. It also identifies exclusionary practices of neoliberal reformers during reform development, political behavior not found in Schickler's work based on the United States.

This study shows specifically that the influence of ideologies, interest groups, and international pressures on Polish policy actors pushed reform in different directions and produced many unintended consequences. In this case, conflicting ideologies and pressures on policy actors stemming from a variety of historical, institutional, political, and international sources resulted in compromises made by the ruling parliamentary coalition. Most significant for immediate outcomes was the tension between neoliberal and neotraditional ideologies espoused by reformers. Such compromise and tension during reform development was in part responsible for unfavorable public service outcomes. In this study I test the result of these unintended consequences of the politics of reform on outcomes for social service delivery in new provinces and counties. Among other data, I use results from a nationwide, representative survey of Polish public social service offices on three levels of government that I conducted in summer, 2000. The survey provided information on degree of reform implementation, funding levels, civil society activity (including involvement of nongovernmental organizations), professionalization of the social service sector, and intergovernmental cooperation and coordination.

The overriding objective of this study is to show how the politics of decentralization in Poland shaped the reform package and affected social service outcomes on county and provincial levels. It examines what happened to policy goals as they moved through the political process and were written as policy. It then takes the analysis a step further by examining what happened as policy moved through the implementation phase and emerged in the form of outcomes. Analysis of these two phases is key because the ironies of decentralization reform in Poland occurred not only where inconsistencies between goals and written policy resulted in unmet goals but also where consistent goals and policies resulted in unintended outcomes because they worked at cross-purposes with other reform policy. By connecting the politics of decentralization with decentralization outcomes, this research bridges the divide in the decentralization literature between politics and outcomes. In particular, this study not only outlines how politics contributed to decentralization policy that failed to meet its ends but shows more generally that attention to politics is needed when approaching policy reform.[6]

Background

At the beginning of Poland's transition to democracy, decentralization reforms in 1990 transferred decision-making authority to elected municipal governments *(gminy)* and passed down central government tasks and some revenue-raising authority. Despite some problems with the underfunding of decentralized tasks, the municipal reforms were largely deemed a success.[7] Even as municipal reforms were taking place, reformers were thinking of the next stage of public administration reform—the return of the county *(powiat)* level of government and the establishment of large provinces *(województwa)*.[8] Counties and large provinces had been abolished by the Polish communist party in 1975 and replaced by forty-nine small provinces in an effort to enhance state centralization.[9] The provincial administration, an arm of the central government, was considered saturated with communist-era bureaucrats. In addition, there was increasing pressure, much of which was self-imposed, to harmonize Poland's administrative structure with that of Western Europe by creating fewer and larger provinces. The return of counties, on the other hand, was an act to restore the Polish state-administrative structure to its rightful design and give shape once again to the cultural identity formed in these smaller regions over hundreds of years. As shown, however, this second round of reforms fell short of the basic goals Poles had for decentralization, particularly in the areas of democratization and improved public services.

The 1999 public administration reform differed significantly from the 1990 reform in its breadth and depth. The 1990 reform involved decentralization of central government tasks and authority to established municipalities and the organization of 268 administrative regions *(rejony)* drawn roughly along the lines of counties in existence before 1975.[10] The second round in 1999 was considerably more complicated as it sought to dramatically redesign the territorial division of the state and correct a fragmented system of central government administration at the same time as it decentralized tasks and authority. Before the 1999 reform there were forty-nine centrally governed provinces and 2,489 self-governed municipalities with 268 administrative regions. Also in existence were over forty so-called "special administrations" *(administracje specjalne)*—field offices of central ministries and institutions (such as labor offices) that often operated in their own territorial divisions.[11] The reform proposed to liquidate the forty-nine provinces, administrative regions, and special administrations and establish in their stead sixteen large provinces, with both self-government and central government administrations, and 373 self-governed counties (including sixty-five cities with county status).

Most significant, this study of the second round of public administration reforms also finds Poland and its politics under much different circumstances than the first round. The 1990 *Law on Local Government* was passed by a "contract" parliament established in negotiations between the communist party and the Solidarity Trade Union. In this semi-democratic forum, one-third of the seats in the lower house of parliament (Sejm) and all of the Senate seats were opened to free democratic elections and were subsequently won by Solidarity. Solidarity showed a unified front and won against the communist party, who opposed local government reform on ideological and practical grounds. For communists, the reforms undermined the principle of unified state authority and cut off their control of the local level. In addition, rigid communist bureaucrats resisted any change in their sphere of control and authority. Indeed, one of the main goals of reformers at that time was to establish a democratic stronghold on the local level to counterbalance waning, though still pervasive, communist control in the central government.[12]

Influences on Reform

At the time of the second round of public administration reform, the fully democratic parliamentary elections of 1998 had just removed the Democratic Left Alliance (SLD), the left-leaning former communist party in control of the government for four years, and placed in power a tenuous coalition government made up of the Solidarity Electoral Action (AWS) and the Freedom Union (UW). These two center-right parties had large differences both between themselves and within their own parties as to the means and ends of many aspects of state policy, including public administration reform. In addition, central bureaucracies were again on the defensive, not wanting to give up more control and authority after losing a fair share in the municipal reforms. Old provincial capital cities, often politically powerful, also resisted the loss in status that would inevitably come with the abolishment of many of the old forty-nine provinces. Reformers were also more aware of the Western international community to which it wanted to belong and that had much more interest in Poland's designs for public administration than previously. Western ideologies on decentralization and fiscal matters had also had more time to settle into the experience and thinking of policy actors involved in reform development. In this study, I argue that it is the influence of these ideologies, interest groups, and international pressures on policy actors that pushed reform in different directions and produced many unintended consequences.

Ideologies

Neotraditionalism in the Polish postcommunist context refers to a general attitude that changes attributed to the communist party that significantly altered the "Polish" state of affairs were things that needed to be undone, "fixed," and restored to their original "natural" state. In this case it was a return to the decentralized system and territorial division of the state that had been in place before communism. Restoration of self-governing counties that had been abolished by the communist party in 1975 was especially viewed as an important step in returning Poland to its rightful democratic structure. Counties themselves were viewed as "small fatherlands" *(małe ojczyzny)* with their own cultural identities that deserved the right to self-government almost as much as Poland as a country deserved this right. It was in counties that reformers of the second round of decentralization had hope for a further renewal of civil society. This return to a historical public administration design, though most heavily influential in counties and county government, was influential in other aspects of the reform, as well.[13]

Administrative, political, and fiscal decentralization broadly construed were supported by another neotraditional tendency, a return to allowing into state matters principles espoused by the Catholic Church. The Catholic Church in Poland provided support for the idea of *pomocniczość* or, roughly translated, subsidiarity, the idea that the smallest unit possible should provide assistance on behalf of the citizen. The Church's position on *pomocniczość* is found in the Centesimus Annus encyclical (1991) and defines it as follows: "The society of the highest level of government should not interfere in the internal matters of the society of the lowest level, depriving it of its jurisdiction, but rather it should support it in cases of necessity and help in the coordination of activities with activities of other social groups, for the common good."[14] A Polish reformer states, "The principle of 'pomocniczość,' traced back to the Old Testament and developed by the social teachings of the [Catholic] Church, is presently accepted as one of the foundations of democratic state structure."[15] Indeed, *pomocniczość* is explicitly stated in the preamble of the new Polish constitution as one of the principles of the Polish system.[16]

Neotraditionalism was an ideology espoused by policy actors who were the initiators of the reform. They included parliamentary representatives who had worked in local government and had the continuation of decentralization as their specific goal when they entered parliament in 1998. In the Solidarity Electoral Action party alone there were over seventy members of parliament who were previously or currently mayors or councilmen on the municipal level.[17] They came to be known as "self-governmenters" *(samorządowcy)* and were found mostly in the governing right coalition but also among representatives of the Democratic Left Alliance.[18] Initiators were also found among government officials and academics who had long worked on the problem of decentralization and public administration reform in Poland.

Another ideology found in policy actors in the right coalition was neoliberalism. During the early years of transition, neoliberalism was a predominant ideology guiding the transition to democracy and a free market in East Central Europe. The economic prescription called for stabilization that reduced government subsidies and limited budget deficit, price and trade liberalization, privatization, and, institutionally, an overall withdrawal of the state from the economy. In a democracy it was believed that such a course would inevitably be resisted by those who stood to lose at the outset. Thus, while supporting democracy as a principle, neoliberals worked to restrict the development of reforms to economists who were politically insulated from the democratic process. Indeed, reforms were to be a painful but quick process after which the economy would stabilize and everyone would be much better off for having gone through it. This was seen as a more desirable alternative to extended reforms that would result in longer but more moderate suffering but not deliver quick positive returns. In the postcommunist world, neoliberals believed there was a window of opportunity immediately after the fall of the communist regime when support for democracy and new reforms was high, and citizens would tolerate the unemployment and steep drop in the standard of living brought on by extensive and quick economic reform.[19]

Poland in particular embraced neoliberalism not only in content but also in policy approach. Leszek Balcerowicz, the Polish minister of finance (1989–91), and a small team of technocrats, including foreign advisors, drew up plans for quick restructuring of the Polish economy—an idea known as "shock therapy." Society's awareness of the need for reform due to the economic crisis in Poland, a supportive parliament, and the blessing of the Solidarity movement provided the political insulation Balcerowicz's team needed to prepare an economic package with little outside interference and have it passed quickly into law.[20] This was the experience neoliberals had with policy making and set a precedent for when Leszek Balcerowicz and other neoliberals returned to the Ministry of Finance in fall, 1998, and began work on four large reforms, the public administration reform among them. Neoliberals closely involved with the public administration reform from a fiscal standpoint were successful in their closed-door policy and also in their efforts to keep public funds on the central level while divesting the central government of public responsibilities. Such conduct resulted in serious negative consequences for the entire public administration reform. Neoliberal inclinations were partly to blame for why fiscal decentralization did not take place as planned and mainly responsible for a temporary fiscal plan that failed to adequately fund newly decentralized tasks and services.

The necessity for haste in the reform process was one element of neoliberalism that center-right reformers, both members of parliament and government officials, espoused across the board when they returned to power in 1997. Indeed, only a little over a year was planned to finish work on the administrative reform and push it through the legislative process. In terms of work on administrative decentralization alone, this meant the amendment of almost two hundred existing laws.[21] Reformers generally accepted an approach to the policymaking process that worked to achieve consensus as quickly as possible by proposing general, imprecise reform solutions with modifications made during implementation under the guidance of real experience. But the haste of reformers was heavily if not mainly influenced by their perception of the political context. Much emphasis was placed on the fact that political will to proceed with the reform was present when the right came into power in the fall of 1997 but might diminish over time.[22] That is, they again viewed the wave of popularity that brought them into power as a window of opportunity during which it was possible to pass difficult reform measures. Moreover, it was thought political will would diminish specifically among supporters in parliament because it was believed the more time representatives spent in Warsaw the more they would come under the influence of central ministers resistant to reform.[23] Reformers also wanted to make use of the element of surprise, thinking that if reforms were done fast enough those against them would not have time to organize resistance.[24] This attempt to shield reform from interest group reaction was a typical neoliberal move. In this case it was of particular importance with regard to central ministries who would resist decentralization. It was also thought reforms needed to be passed as quickly as possible so that positive outcomes could be experienced before the next parliamentary elections.[25] The right's ideology of policymaking, that of hasty preparation, was later blamed in part for unclear and inconsistent legislation and poor initial outcomes, an effect of neoliberal thinking that was not limited to fiscal aspects of reform development.[26]

Interest Groups

Interest groups sprang up almost immediately to block aspects of the reform or to promote a version of the reform more beneficial to their interests. These groups consisted of central bureaucrats, trade unions, and defenders of old provincial capitals, county advocates, and local government associations. Reform and removal of the old communist bureaucratic apparatus was a priority for reformers for political reasons: to decommunize the administrative bureaucracy and put government responsibilities more directly under control of the people (though this was also motivated by neotraditionalism). Administrative decentralization was intended to not only decentralize many ministerial tasks but also dismantle deconcentrated special administrations that existed on the level of newly proposed counties and were directly subordinate to the ministries. Many ministerial duties and special administrations were to be transferred to elected county and provincial governments, which meant they were taken out of the hands of old party bureaucrats and put under control of the people.

Given this pointed attack on the existent public administration system it was no wonder central bureaucracies put up considerable resistance during reform development. Well-entrenched ministries were reluctant to have their responsibilities and funds decentralized to lower levels of government and fought any kind of restructuring of the central administration at the center. Loss of control over ministerial tasks and deconcentrated special administrations and funds for them meant a significant loss of jobs and power for ministries. Among central ministries there was also the mentality that if an administrative task was important it should stay in the hands of the state administration and not be passed to "incompetent" locally elected officials. Interestingly, ministers were in favor of decentralization in general but not when it came to their own ministry; each felt his or her ministry should be the exception. Outcomes in this area thus differed largely according to the political influence of a given ministry and the willingness of reformers to compromise in their demands in exchange for a minister's support of the reform as a whole.[27]

Several trade unions were also staunchly opposed to administrative decentralization in their respective areas. Administrative and political decentralization for them meant loss of influence over issues currently controlled in the center and thus also loss of bargaining power with the central government. Two unions in particular, the Solidarity Labor Union and the Polish Teachers Union (Związek Nauczycielstwa Polskiego), were able to significantly influence the reform process in the area of decentralization though with differing degrees of impact on outcomes.

A strong lobby was also created by inhabitants of old provincial capitals that stood to lose their status with the reform. Reformers initially established the optimal number of provinces at twelve, which meant the abolishment of thirty-seven provincial capitals. Residents of these capitals feared the loss of jobs and resources that would follow and protested by organizing rallies in front of parliament and in extreme cases by blocking roads and railway lines.[28] Such pressure was largely responsible for the establishment of sixteen rather than twelve provinces and resulted in compensation to abolished provincial capitals, such as giving them status as both municipalities and counties.

There were also numerous county groups that sprang up to promote the return or creation of a county in their area. These groups traveled to Warsaw and petitioned parliamentary committees directly for their counties. Lawmakers, in their quest for political support, all too often acquiesced to their requests even though it pushed the number of counties far beyond the recommended number.

Local government organizations on the national level were eager advocates of the public administration reform supporting the decentralization of functions and authority to lower levels of government. Such organizations included the Union of Metropolitan Cities, the Association of Rural Municipalities, the Union of Polish Towns, and the Association of Polish Cities, among others. Most notable about their role in the reform process, however, was their inability to effect real change in the most important areas. Local government organizations were too weak to monitor the reform of local government finances; indeed, local government representatives were consistently left out of policymaking for fiscal reforms that had a large impact on local government.[29] Nonetheless, such supportive organizations played an important behind-the-scenes role during the years leading up to and after the 1999 reform through their work organizing training, conferences, consultation services, research on local government, and lobby efforts.[30]

International Influence

International influence on the public administration reform came in various forms. First, there was the soft influence of Western ideologies and ideas that were adopted by reformers. This included neoliberalism espoused by foreign advisors to Poland from the early transition period but also supported by more long-term players such as the World Bank and the International Monetary Fund (IMF). Ideas on decentralization, especially in terms of subsidiarity, were put forward by the European Union (EU) and indirectly encouraged in country assessments. A host of other international organizations were influential in their dissemination of ideas about and support for decentralization. The U.S. Agency for International Development (USAID) funded full-time American advisors and other consultants to work with reformers, most significantly the Ministry of Finance, on developing legislation for fiscal decentralization (though advice in this area went largely unused). Other technical assistance for the reform, including expert conferences and study trips to West European countries, was provided by International Policy Services (contracted by the Commission of European Communities), the International Investment Fund, the World Bank, DATAR (department of the French government), the French-Polish Foundation, the Swedish Agency of International Development, and the British Know How Fund. The EU's PHARE program eventually funded training for local governments and monitoring and analysis of the reform.[31]

Second, there existed a kind of international influence of the carrot variety. That is, European Union aid in the form of structural assistance and the ability to compete economically on the same level with other large regions in Western Europe were great incentives for Poland to create a complementary regional system. A third type of international influence on the reforms came in the more direct form of the Council of Europe's charters on local and regional government, signed by Poland, which directly call for elected self-governments on subnational levels.

Politics and Outcomes of Decentralization

This study bridges a divide in the decentralization literature between politics and outcomes by showing how the politics of decentralization affect social service outcomes. In particular, it addresses a narrow focus in the decentralization outcomes literature on expected consequences of decentralization (whether positive or negative) that overlooks the unintended consequences that stem from the politics of decentralization. Polish reformers attempted to develop and implement policies in line with decentralization literature that claimed positive results of reform. In practice, however, they found that both development and implementation of such decentralization policy were compromised by the politics of reform.[32]

As stated, the literature on decentralization consists of two separate forums. The first focuses on the politics of decentralization in terms of why decentralization or a certain degree of decentralization takes place in a given country or countries.[33] The second looks at the outcomes of decentralization policy concentrating on fiscal arrangements[34] and good governance in terms of gains or losses to democracy and efficiency as a result of decentralization.[35] Much of the democratic outcomes literature focuses on the responsiveness and participation of those on the local level after decentralization.[36] The study of the outcomes of decentralization also includes a number of publications on lessons learned from decentralization or conditions for its success also largely measured in terms of improvement to democracy and efficiency.[37] In addition, there are many mostly descriptive accounts of decentralization undertaken in various countries.[38] Largely missing from the decentralization literature is work connecting the politics of decentralization with specific outcomes for public services on subnational levels. The following is an overview of these two separate literatures in the areas relevant to this study: the politics of public administration reform in East Central Europe and decentralization outcomes for public services.

Politics of Public Administration Reform in East Central Europe
The current literature on public administration reform in East Central Europe falls generally into two categories: outlines of the political determinants of reform or largely descriptive accounts of the new public administration system in a given country or countries.[39] Those addressing the politics of public administration reform focus on the identification of various explanatory concepts or main variables of change, including historical legacies (precommunist, communist, and sometimes postcommunist), ideas or ideology of main actors, and geographic considerations. Martin Brusis, in his comparative analysis of administrative reform in six postcommunist countries, uses historical legacies, policy approaches, and historical and ethnic regionalism. Illner identifies four "contextual factors," including precommunist and communist legacies, the political context of the reforms, expectations toward decentralization, and geographic and demographic factors. Hesse uses as many as six such variables.[40] Wollman frames his analysis around an institutionalist approach that looks at "institution building as a sequence of institutional choices." He identifies many of the same contextual factors as others to explain why certain institutional choices were made.[41] This literature is largely focused on outputs of political decentralization and state territorial division (in other words, the type of subgovernment established and the final size and number of new subnational units) and overlooks administrative and fiscal decentralization and, most significantly, reform outcomes generally (the

actual functioning of the new system). Or it focuses almost solely on fiscal decentralization with only cursory attention to other aspects of the reform.[42]

Decentralization Outcomes for Public Services

The decentralization outcomes literature discusses outcomes in terms of the effect decentralization is expected to have on democracy and efficiency. However, it provides a mixed explanation of the effect decentralization should have in these two areas. The central claim of proponents of decentralization is that decentralization improves democracy because it brings government closer to the people. Closer government means citizens have more opportunity to participate in decisions affecting their lives; they are also better able to hold government representatives accountable for their actions. Decentralization is also said to make possible minority representation when the majority at the center makes it difficult for minority interests to be represented on the national level. This is especially salient when a minority on the national level is a majority on the local level.[43]

In the area of public services some of the outcomes literature claims the benefits of improved democracy by noting that services more closely match the needs of citizens, public institutions are more responsive to changes in those needs, and such change results in innovative approaches that may be applied on a wider basis. It also points out that increased government accountability allows for citizens to hold representatives accountable for problems with services and encourages quality from the start. Also, minorities are better able to advocate for services they need when they are a majority on the local level.[44]

Other literature argues, however, that decentralization takes away from another type of democracy found in the concept of social citizenship. Social citizenship is the idea that every citizen is entitled to a minimum level of social goods by virtue of his or her membership in the polity regardless of place of residence.[45] Decentralization limits the egalitarian distribution of public resources made possible by centralization and opens the door for disparity and a general reduction in services.[46] When funding responsibility is decentralized, localities compete to keep taxes low to attract business as well as to avoid becoming "welfare magnets." Such competition is said to result in a "race to the bottom" as each locality tries to keep taxes and services lower with respect to other localities.[47] However, there is ongoing debate over the validity of this argument.[48] Centralization is also said to protect the rights of minorities on the local level from local majorities that might discriminate in the delivery of social services.[49]

In terms of outcomes for efficiency, some of the decentralization literature claims it creates a more efficient system mainly because subnational governments are familiar with local economic and social conditions and can therefore administer programs more efficiently. Elements of decentralized democracy, such as improved accountability and responsiveness of local governments, also work to improve efficiency. Research on economies of scale shows that for more *labor-intensive* services, decentralization to many small units of government may be more efficient than administration by larger, centralized units.[50] Other literature, however, argues that decentralization takes away the efficiency that comes with a centralized system, which includes consolidation and coordination of planning, elimination of overlapping jurisdictions and service duplication, and the provision of an economy of scale. Indeed, for *capital-intensive* services, some authors posit that larger, more centralized units of government create a more efficient economy of scale than many small decentralized units.[51]

Many of the benefits and limitations of decentralization as outlined above are contingent on the type of decentralization instituted. There are three basic types of decentralization: devolution as the transfer of fiscal and administrative responsibilities from the central government to subnational governments; delegation as the transfer of administrative responsibility for service provision to subnational governments with fiscal responsibility remaining with the central government; deconcentration as the extension of the central government through regional branches that have little or no decision-making authority. The Western literature holds that most of the benefits (and limitations) of decentralization come with devolution, where subnational governments are given fiscal and administrative control over a set of public responsibilities.[52]

The Polish case shows that decentralization in practice is not as straightforward as decentralization in theory. While governments may attempt to follow decentralization recommendations that they expect will result in specific outcomes, the reality is that they are often constrained by different influences on reform that ultimately lead to unintended consequences. Polish policy actors were unable to attain an elusive balance in policy that they believed would simultaneously provide benefits to democracy and efficiency. As will be shown, the culture and policy environment in Poland at the time of the reform resulted in policies that favored democratization over efficiency when the two came in conflict. Reformers essentially lacked the political power to force a golden middle ground between the two and, indeed, compromised it in order to get the reform passed at all.

Research Strategy and Methods

This analysis uses an in-depth case study of decentralization reform in Poland as a research strategy that employs the data collection methods of focused interviews and self-administered questionnaires. A case study of one country was chosen because the topic indicated an in-depth case study of one country over a more superficial study of several countries. The case study strategy "is an empirical inquiry that investigates a contemporary phenomenon within its real-life context."[53] This study examines reform outcomes in the political context of reform development.

Poland was chosen as the country of study because it was among the first of the East Central European countries to introduce midlevel decentralization. Moreover, it instituted both counties and self-governing provinces whereas other countries in the region had only one or the other in place at the time of the study.[54] Thus, a study of Poland as a forerunner in this area provides valuable information for other countries anticipating similar reforms. It also provides a comprehensive knowledge base for this type of reform against which reforms in other East Central European countries can be compared.

The study's focus on both the politics of decentralization reform and its service outcomes necessitated the use of two different types of original data collection: focused interviews were used to understand the politics of reform, and survey questionnaires were used to assess outcomes. Focused interviews were conducted to collect data on the politics of the reform for several reasons. First, detailed information was needed on a subject for which there was little information available. Second, the insights of particular reformers on specific aspects of the reform were sought after. Third, access to other potential interviewees was provided through contact with each successive interviewee.[55] In 2000–2001, a total of twenty-three interviews were conducted with important reform actors. Twelve interviews were conducted with eleven members of the Polish parliament representing the four main political parties. Eleven interviews were conducted with eight government officials and one university professor who were directly involved in the reform. Most of the government officials interviewed held high positions in central ministries at the time of reform development, including the Ministry of Internal Affairs and Administration, the Ministry of Finance, and the Ministry of Labor and Social Policy. Also, two interviews were with the head of the reform: the former secretary of state and government plenipotentiary for state systemic reform.

Data collection on reform outcomes in the area of social services necessitated a different approach. The goal was to obtain a nationwide picture of social service delivery after the reform to test hypotheses generated from a preliminary survey questionnaire. To achieve this goal, a nationwide representative survey was conducted during summer, 2000, of directors of two hundred public social service institutions on three levels of government. Institutions in the study included sixty-six municipal social assistance centers, seventy county family assistance centers, thirty-two city family assistance centers, all sixteen provincial departments of social affairs and all sixteen provincial regional social policy centers. On county and provincial levels, self-administered questionnaires consisting of close-ended questions were delivered by an interviewer who remained present during survey completion. Surveys conducted in municipalities were done by computer-assisted telephone interviewing (CATI) using fixed-response questions.[56] A Polish research institute, Pracownia Badań Społecznych, provided trained interviewers and initial data analysis.[57] Research was conducted one and a half years after reform implementation first began in January, 1999; expectations for outcomes were thus moderated against the early timing of the study.[58] Document collection was also undertaken to supplement the original research on politics and outcomes of the reform.

The social service sector was selected for analysis for a variety of reasons. Most decentralization research on social services focuses on the education and health sectors and leaves out other important services such as those for the mentally and physically disabled, orphans, families in crisis, juvenile delinquents, and the elderly. This research focuses specifically on these overlooked services often administered by midlevel government. Also important, this mix of services provides an interesting array of program and funding types, which makes it possible to analyze the effect of decentralization in a variety of circumstances. Lessons learned from analysis of the decentralization of these programs can potentially be applied to similar program types in other sectors.

A question may arise as to the need to conduct research on social service decentralization reform when it is widely held that decentralization of social services leads to regional disparities and decreasing funding of services for the poor.[59] Paul Peterson states rather conclusively, "To recommend that the provision of welfare should be locally controlled and its marginal cost borne by state and local taxpayers is to recommend that the poor be all but abandoned."[60] The purpose of this project, however, is not to test or repeat studies evaluating the economic outcome of fiscal decentralization. Indeed, an exact test of the redistributive policy thesis was not possible because true decentralization of fiscal responsibility to subnational levels, though expected, did not happen in Poland.[61] The aim of the study is, however, to analyze social service outcomes against a broad range of goals held by Polish reformers. In any case, the Polish point of view on the tendency of fiscal decentralization to introduce disparity differed from those of Western decentralization scholars due to long experience with a centralized system that did not adequately or fairly distribute resources. Indeed, Polish reformers believed that a decentralized system directly overseen by citizens would lead to better services and that equalization measures between wealthy and poor subnational units could address disparities.[62] This hypothesis, however, can only be tested once fiscal decentralization occurs.

2 Historical Background
Counties and Provinces in Poland

The 1999 public administration reform has its roots deep in Poland's history. Mid-level territorial division in Poland dates back to the twelfth and thirteenth centuries when provinces of the Polish lands grew to prominence. During this "period of fragmentation" of the Polish kingdom, provinces became increasingly self-sufficient and well-defined.[1] Three later historical periods are most relevant for the modern development and shape of county and provincial units in the Polish state: the Polish-Lithuanian Commonwealth (1569–1795), the Second Republic of Poland (1918–39), and the Third Republic of People's Poland (1944–89).[2] Also salient are post-1989 proposals and debates on the (re)construction of mid-level territorial units that preceded the 1999 public administration reform.

Brief History of Counties and Provinces in Poland

The period of the Polish-Lithuanian Commonwealth was characterized by strong provinces and traditional counties. With the creation of the Commonwealth in 1569, twenty-two provinces were established in the Polish Crown and ten in the Grand Duchy of Lithuania (see map 2). The head of a province was nominated by the king from among the province's aristocratic families and also served as a member of the Polish Senate. The provinces had strong territorial identities and were increasingly dominated by powerful aristocratic families. Over time they became more a unit of self-government of the nobility than a unit of state administration. The provincial division of 1569 endured until 1772 when parts of the Commonwealth came under foreign domination. In the Polish Crown, provinces were often divided into counties known as *ziemia* that had roots in former principalities of the twelfth and thirteenth centuries. Each *ziemia* had its own courts, administration, and elected assembly. The Lithuanian equivalent of the *ziemia* was the *powiat,* introduced immediately preceding the creation of the Commonwealth as a more systematic territorial-administrative division. In the Polish Crown, the *powiat* was strictly an administrative unit

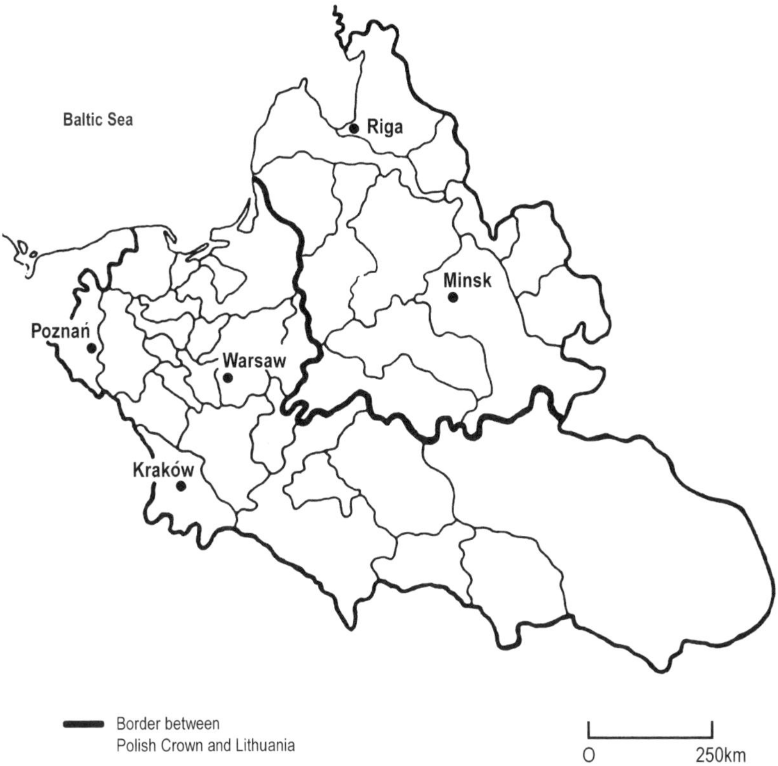

Map 2. Provincial division of Poland in the sixteenth century. Source: Antoni Kuklinski and P. Swianiewicz, "The Polish Palatinatus: Experiences and Prospects," in *The Rise of Meso Government in Europe.*

established for the purpose of noble tribunals and, later, tax and administration.[3]

From 1795 to 1918 the Polish and Lithuanian territories were under the domination of Russia, Austria, and Prussia. Each of those countries instituted different territorial divisions in their occupied part of Poland. These divisions persisted during most of the period of the Second Republic of Poland, 1918–39. In lands dominated by Russia, limited self-governing rural municipalities (introduced in 1864) were made up of several villages that also had their own elected bodies. Urban municipal and county self-governments were only introduced during World War I under Austrian and German occupation. In each of two regions formerly occupied by Austria (Galicia and Austrian Silesia), a type of regional assembly (Sejm Krajowy) operated that was based on a complicated and largely undemocratic system of electoral colleges.[4] The assembly selected members of an executive department (Wydział Krajowy) that, among other responsibilities, oversaw local government. Each region had different arrangements for municipal and county *(powiat)* self-government. The main difference was that the Austria Silesia region, as opposed to other regions, lacked county self-government. Lands under Prussian rule had three levels of self-government. Municipalities generally included only one town, counties *(powiaty)* were small, and provinces had both a central government provincial branch and an elected assembly. In the first years of Poland's independence a number of separate laws introduced more democratic elections and functioning of municipal and county self-government specific to each of the three formerly occupied areas.[5]

After several attempts at unifying this disparate system, a 1933 law unified the municipal and county levels of government in name and function. However, the new structure somewhat limited subnational self-government, reflecting a change from a parliamentary democracy to a semi-autocratic state that occurred after the overthrow of the government in 1926. Rural and urban municipalities and counties *(powiaty)*—there were 264 counties before World War II—were given greater administrative responsibilities but fewer lawmaking powers. Similarly, the boundaries of the sixteen large provinces *(województwa)* created in 1938 followed historic tradition, but there was no provision for an elected provincial assembly (see map 3). Exceptions were the elected provincial assemblies still operating in three provinces of the former Prussian partition. The head of a province was nominated by the president of Poland and was largely a representative of the central government. This official headed up a provincial administration and had strong oversight over local governments. An exception to this was the Silesian province, which had been granted a certain level of autonomy from the central government (the Silesian province was made up of parts of the former Prussian Upper Silesia and the Polish portion of the old Austrian Silesia). These changes to the administrative-territorial division of the country were disrupted with the advent of World War II in 1939.[6]

After 1944 Soviet domination in Poland initially allowed prewar subnational divisions and institutions to endure; later reforms,

Map 3. Provincial division of Poland late in the Second Republic, 1938 (sixteen provinces). Source: Antoni Kuklinski and P. Swianiewicz, "The Polish Palatinatus: Experiences and Prospects," in *The Rise of Meso Government in Europe.*

however, completely dismantled the traditional boundaries and institutions of regional and local governments. For the first six years, communist party officials re-instituted the pre-existing structure of counties and municipalities, even extending this system to land recovered from Germany. Remarkably there was an increase in regional self-government with the establishment of elected provincial assemblies alongside central government institutions. Fourteen provinces were shaped out of the new territorial boundaries of Poland (following old provincial regions where possible), and 299 counties *(powiaty)* were created (see map 4). This arrangement, however, was short-lived.[7]

Map 4. Provincial division of Poland following World War II, 1946 (fourteen provinces). Source: Jerzy Regulski, *Samorząd III Rzeczypospolitej.*

With the growing influence of the communist party, sweeping changes were subsequently made to subnational institutions. In 1950 the party replaced subnational self-governments with a system of councils *(rady narodowe)* in line with the Soviet philosophy of "democratic centralism" and controlled by the communist party.[8] Lower councils were subordinate to higher councils, which assured the dominance of the central governing council, and many responsibilities were centralized. Changes were also made to the territorial division of the country. By 1955 there were 17 provinces, 371 counties *(powiaty)* and, in place of municipalities, numerous, smaller districts *(gromady)* (see map 5). The most dramatic change in territorial arrangement, however, came during 1972–75. In an

Map 5. Provincial division of Poland, 1950–75 (seventeen provinces). Source: Jerzy Regulski, *Samorząd III Rzeczypospolitej.*

effort to undermine the growing influence of provincial officials and deepen the reach of the central government, the communist party abolished the existing provincial and county levels, replaced them with one level of 49 provinces, and restored municipalities (see map 6).[9]

The history of Poland's administrative divisions leading up to 1989 would be incomplete without reference to a significant socioeconomic division of the country along east-west lines. Dating back to the beginning of Poland's history, the Vistula River has been the informal dividing line between a more developed and prosperous western territory and a less developed, poor eastern region. Over

Map 6. Provincial division of Poland, 1975–98 (forty-nine provinces). Source: Jerzy Regulski, *Samorząd III Rzeczypospolitej.*

time western Poland has benefited from its proximity to Western Europe, beginning with its inclusion in the first wave of urban development between the thirteenth and fifteenth centuries. Later, industrialization took place to a greater degree in the west than in the east. With the Prussian occupation of western Poland during the nineteenth century, the region found itself part of a rapidly modernizing and well-ordered European state. Meanwhile, the lands under Russian domination in the east fell further behind. In communist Poland, despite a policy to equalize regional differences, major economic centers were often located in areas already on the path of industrialization. The eastern territories, often referred to as "Poland B" or the "Eastern Wall," remain less developed and largely rural to the present day.[10]

Post-1989 Attempts at County and Provincial Reform

With the fall of the Polish communist party in 1989 the door was opened for a reorganization of the subnational system of government. By March, 1990, Solidarity reformers had passed the *Law on Local Government* that restored self-government to the municipal level and provided it with substantial financial and administrative autonomy. The 1990 reforms also established the purely administrative *rejon* unit between the county and provincial levels. The success of municipal reforms, despite some underfunding of decentralized responsibilities, later provided support for county and provincial reforms.[11] Reformers planned to start with municipal reforms to establish a strong foundation and then, within two years, continue with reforms on other levels. County and provincial reforms were clearly viewed as a continuation and completion of the first round of local government reform.[12]

Indeed, the return of the county level of government, abolished by the communist party in 1975, was on the minds of some Solidarity reformers at the end of 1989 even before work on the municipal reform began. Many felt the destruction of the county level was an act that hit at the very heart of the identity of the state as "the administrative structure is also an ingredient of the nation's culture."[13] Organized counties had been in existence since the beginning of the Commonwealth and had endured through successive changes in the political landscape until 1975. In addition, restoration of the counties was seen as "the master key" to reshaping a highly centralized system of fragmented central government administration found then on the middle levels of government (including the old provincial level and the new administrative *rejon* level below that). Reformers also looked at county and provincial reforms as a convenient and necessary way to rid the provincial and *rejon* apparatus of its communist-era work force.[14]

The first propositions for regional change came during the government of Premier Jan Krzysztof Bielecki. In power after the resignation of Tadeusz Mazowiecki in the fall of 1990, Bielecki proposed the liquidation of newly established *rejony,* the creation of a second county tier of government in their place, and the regionalization of the country. While there had been calls for the return of counties when the *rejony* had been created, this was the first time a serious proposal for regionalization had been made. Plans called for the creation of regions with self-elected regional governments equipped with legislative competencies as well as a regional central government presence. This regional structure was based on the German *Länder* model and was tied to a federalist system. As such, it met with much resistance from those who sought to keep Poland a unitary state as well as from those who were afraid it would be the first step in the subordination of Poland to German influence, leading eventually to loss of sovereignty. As a result, the reform project changed its focus to the creation of ten to twelve large provinces with a central government administration only. It was also in Bielecki's working groups that the idea first arose for counties to be established from the bottom up as associations of municipalities. The work of these groups, however, did not lead to any specific legislation in 1991, which some blame on a lack of conceptualization for the reform as well as lack of courage on the part of the political elite. Others look to the political difficulties of the time, especially preparations for the first democratic elections to parliament and political barriers to the reform as a reason for legislative inaction.[15] Other interpretations of Bielecki's work during this period doubt his interest in promoting decentralization per se and assert his real focus was on the creation of strong regional governments that could realize his objectives for economic reform.[16]

With the parliamentary elections in the fall of 1991 a succession of premiers and their governments made it difficult to push through reforms even when there was the political will and preparation to do so. The Olszewski government (1991–92) returned the emphasis of public administration reform to a focus on local government and considered its role in relation to the role of central government but was not able to advance with serious work on the reform.[17] The Suchocka government (1992–93) placed the most emphasis on continuing the public administration reform, and even though the government lasted only a little over a year much was accomplished that was later used in 1998.[18] Support for the reform was found specifically in Jan Maria Rokita, who at the time was the head of the Office of the Council of Ministers. In October, 1992, Suchocka created the office of the government plenipotentiary for public administration reform and called Michał Kulesza to the past. He was responsible for the entire reform, including the overall strategy, the new administrative division of the country, and legislative projects. One of the main areas of focus was the creation of counties, leaving for later the issue of the creation of large provinces.[19] The Suchocka government had the following main goals for the reform:

1 reform of the state administration in the center and in the field
2 reform of the territorial organization of the country, including the creation of county self-government
3 reform of the state civil service
4 improvement of organizational efficiency in the flow of information and decision-making process
5 improvement in the effective use of public resources[20]

While most preparation was done through expert working groups established by Kulesza, Rokita oversaw the project on state administration reform in the center. Work progressed on each of the goals of the reform and resulted in many concrete legislative projects. Attention was also placed on preparation for provincial reforms that foresaw central government administration in the provinces *without self-government representation.* Plans for twelve, seventeen, and twenty-five provinces were drawn up.[21] The creation of the first map of counties was undertaken immediately by Kulesza in October, 1992. It was guided by the idea that counties should be "historical" in nature and once again form the basic unit of local identity.[22] This work on the territorial division of counties heavily guided county reforms in 1998.

The greatest immediate progress on county reform came with the county pilot project instituted in July, 1993. The program was open to forty-six cities with populations above 100,000. It allowed these cities to voluntarily enter into negotiations with the central government to decentralize selected services planned for the county level. Thirty-four large cities initially made such agreements with the central government. The program, however, was criticized for decentralizing responsibilities without sufficient funds to realize them.[23]

Up until the change of government in the fall of 1993, work also proceeded in forums outside the auspices of government working groups. This included a project on self-governing counties supported by the Democratic Union party but put together by local government representatives. Though received in parliament in January, 1992, its first reading did not take place until a year later in January, 1993. While no further action was taken with the project, it became the basis for legislation on the county government system in 1998.[24]

Parliamentary elections in September, 1993, handed the former communists a majority in parliament, and subsequent efforts to get public administration reform on the parliamentary agenda were blocked for four years. There were several official reasons why the left coalition was opposed to the reform. First, there was a stalemate between the coalition partners: the Democratic Left Alliance (SLD) was in favor of decentralization while the Polish Peasant Party (PSL) was against it. The Polish Peasant Party officially opposed plans for the new administrative structure because the plans were not sound in their view. Unofficially, they were fearful the reform would undermine the party's strong position on the old provincial level and in rural localities, because it would abolish old provinces and restore the county level.[25] Kulesza states that "members of that party [PSL] wanted to retain the small Voivodship [province] where the party apparatus and activists were strong and played a vital role."[26] Second, the coalition believed there was not enough time to prepare the reforms well. It also insisted the Constitution should be passed before administrative reforms were addressed in parliament, which was viewed by reform proponents as a stalling tactic. In fact at the beginning of this period, under Prime Minister Pawlak (1993–95), decentralization reforms already underway were frequently obstructed, including the pilot program for large cities, VAT (value-added tax) compensation for municipalities, and the transfer of primary schools to municipalities.[27]

Work on the reforms themselves continued in parliamentary committees, outside institutions, and even eventually by the left government in the form of a task force on regional development, in spite of the ongoing blockade in parliament itself. Headed now by former minister Jan Maria Rokita, the Institute of Public Affairs was founded and became one of the more influential of these institutions with regard to the reform. It was established using foreign funds to continue the right's work on public reforms with the goal of being prepared when the right returned to power.[28] The

Institute's Public Administration Reform Program focused mainly on provincial reforms but supported the development of counties along the lines described above. Its main achievement was a project developing a double system of self-government and central government administration on the provincial level. A project to determine the ideal number and division of provinces was conducted in the Center for Social and Economic Research (CASE).[29]

The Center for Local Government and Development based at the University of Warsaw also received foreign funds for research on public administration reform.[30] Under the direction of Professor Andrzej Piekara, it concurrently developed an entirely different project that did not restore the county level along historical lines but left the forty-nine old provinces intact, added to them the forty-six large cities from the pilot project, and labeled them all counties.[31] Following the French model, this project envisioned municipalities coming together on a voluntary basis to form associations that would work on a level just above the municipality as necessity required. It planned that ten to fourteen macroregions could be formed in a similar manner with counties cooperating amongst themselves to draw regional boundaries. The project, though, was in agreement with the dual system of provincial government proposed by the Institute of Public Affairs. Not surprisingly, the Polish Peasant Party adopted this project and later supported it in parliament, though unsuccessfully.[32]

Though the left did not move reforms along in parliament, they began to see the need to prepare for reforms on the provincial level. In 1995, the left government and the Council of Europe established the Task Force for Regional Development in Poland. The main purpose of the group was to "prepare an outline strategy of regional development for Poland and of recommendations for the Polish government, the realization of which, by using West European experience and achievements, would lead to a growth in the competitiveness of the Polish regions, while at the same time restricting the excessive differentiation of their development."[33] The task force also maintained that provincial government should be autonomous and self-governed and be capable of conducting regional development policy. In fall, 1996, the group presented twenty-one recommendations for provincial reform based on the principle of subsidiarity, but no concrete legislative project ever resulted. On another front, the Ministry of Internal Affairs and Administration established a team of experts in 1996 to continue with the overall public administration reform project. The result of this work was a 1997 report entitled "An Effective, Friendly, Safe State: Program for Decentralization of State Functions and Development of Local Self-Government," which was based on some of the work done in the 1992–93 period and included an estimate of the cost of the reform. However, no legislative project emerged out of this work either.[34]

Though not entertaining large scale reform in parliament, the left coalition agreed to expand the county pilot program through the passage of the Law on Large Cities, implemented in 1996 in a concession to the opposition. The law made it mandatory that specified public services intended for the county level be decentralized to Poland's forty-six largest urban municipalities. These services were paid for by funds transferred from the central government over which municipalities had broad revenue assignment authority.[35]

An important foundation for further public administration reform was outlined in the new Polish Constitution passed in 1997. While establishing Poland as a unitary state, the 1997 Constitution ensured the continued decentralization of authority and tasks in several ways. The principle of *pomocniczość,* the idea that the citizen should be assisted by the smallest appropriate unit possible, was included in the Constitution's preamble. It states, "we hereby establish this Constitution of the Republic of Poland as the basic law for the State based on ... the principle of aiding [*pomocniczość* in Polish] in strengthening the powers of citizens and their communities." Article 15 states, "The territorial system of the Republic of Poland shall ensure the decentralization of public power." Article 16 states specifically that each level of subnational government is to have self-government: "The inhabitants of the units of basic territorial division shall form a self-governing community in accordance with law." In addition, the Constitution establishes that local self-government units "shall be assured public funds adequate for the performance of the duties assigned to them" and provides that any changes in these duties will result in a corresponding change in the share of public revenues (see appendix A for relevant excerpts from the 1997 Constitution of the Republic of Poland).[36]

Proponents of public administration reform, largely from the

Freedom Union party, fought hard to establish within the Constitution a specific number of subnational government levels as well as the provision that the level of government above the municipality be the *powiat* or county. Those against the reform, namely the Polish Peasant Party, refused to allow this concession. Thus, the Constitution sets forth only the municipality by name and requires that other levels of subnational government be established by statute.[37]

Work on public administration reform picked up considerable speed when the right returned to power in the parliamentary elections of fall, 1997. The goal of the right coalition, consisting of the Solidarity Electoral Action (AWS) party and the Freedom Union (UW), was to implement the public administration reform and the pension, education, and health care reforms simultaneously in January, 1999. Among the in-coming parliamentarians were representatives who had worked in local government and had the continuation of decentralization as their specific goal. They came to be known as "self-governmenters" *(samorządowcy)* and cut across both the right and left. In the Solidarity Electoral Action party alone there were over seventy members of parliament who were previously or currently mayors or councilmen on the municipal level. Michał Kulesza was called again as the government plenipotentiary for the public administration reform, and many involved with reform preparation in 1992–93 returned to government positions. Work that had been done on the public administration reform in the interim by left-dominated parliamentary committees was largely discarded, and projects prepared by the right were brought in. Even with these preparations much work remained with little over a year planned to accomplish it.[38]

Goals of the 1999 Public Administration Reform

During the 1997–98 reform development period reformers expanded their goals for public administration reform. Much of the original vision behind the goals came from Solidarity reformers who had developed and implemented Poland's first administrative reform. Unofficially the reforms were seen as a way to continue the dismantling of the old communist bureaucracy. Also unofficially they were based on a desire to restore Poland's territorial structure to its prewar, precommunist state.[39] This longing for prewar arrangements has been referred to as "legal nostalgia" *(nostalgia prawnicza),* a phenomenon apparently not found in other countries of East Central Europe.[40] It forms part of the basis for the ideology of neotraditionalism discussed in chapter 1.

As with the first round, reforms were *officially* undertaken largely on the basis of expected improvements in democracy and efficiency as outlined in western decentralization literature. Zaucha states, "The main purpose in introducing counties is to make the rest of the social service system ... which is now under central control, more efficient and economically sound by putting it under the scrutiny of its own customers and clients."[41] Identified paths to realizing democracy and efficiency through administrative reforms were broader in scope than found in the western literature, perhaps due to the different starting point of decentralization in Poland (that of entrenched centralization) as compared to current administrative reforms in western countries. This is clearly reflected in the goals of the reform presented below. One noticeable addition is the inclusion of a goal for the improvement of civil society specifically. On the other hand, a clear departure from the western literature is the absence of goals to improve minority input. This is due to the fact that Poland's minority populations are very small (the German minority is the largest and amounts to only 0.8 percent of the population). Goals introduced subsequent to the 1990 municipal reforms and in line with western views included improving transparency and the creation of provinces that would complement European Union regions.[42]

Of particular importance to this study was the goal to decentralize public finances such that subnational self-governments would have a significant amount of budget autonomy. For reformers this meant that subnational self-governments, for the most part, would have assignment authority over funds referred to as "own income" *(dochody własne)* as opposed to targeted subsidies *(dotacje)* and block grants *(subwencje)* from the central government. Surprisingly, there was little discussion on how fiscal decentralization might exacerbate existing disparities in poorer regions, especially Poland B. Reformers believed the creation of larger provinces would greatly improve regional policy for poorer areas in Poland B and that equalization subsidies from the central government would help smooth out large inequalities.[43]

Goals of the 1999 reform were outlined in official government publications and ranged from general to specific. General elements of the reform were:

1. introduction of a new three-level basic territorial division
2. establishment of self-government in counties and provinces
3. construction of general administrative authorities and the joining of most of the special administrations under the authority of their organs
4. a new division of public tasks in the state
5. a change in the system of public finance—passing part of the public funds to the discretion of subnational self-governments[44]

More specific goals of the reform were found in a publication by the State Structural Reform Department located in the Chancellory of the President of the Council of Ministers:

1. the continuation of public management decentralization
2. expansion of civil society mechanisms, democracy, and societal control (oversight) of administrative activities
3. the greater effectiveness of institutions providing public services on a nationwide as well as local scale
4. improvement in the rationality of public expenditures[45]
5. reconstruction of the public finance system and improvement of its cohesiveness
6. to bring order to the public administration competency system and a correction in the flow of information
7. creation of instruments to conduct regional politics
8. bring efficiency to central government functioning; modernize central government administration in the center and in the field
9. development of a professional civil service
10. make possible the natural advance of the political elite (from municipal government through county and provincial government to the national level)
11. adaptation of the country's territorial organization to European Union standards[46]

The history of midlevel territorial units in Poland shows overall a precedence for large, centrally governed provinces and self-governing counties. The greatest disruption to this scheme was the enactment of reforms by the communist party in the mid-1970s that created forty-nine provinces and abolished the county level. Solidarity reformers' goals for midlevel reform immediately following the fall of communism focused on returning the Polish state to its previous administrative heritage and ridding the structure of communist-era bureaucrats. Parliamentary domination by the former communists, however, stalled reforms during 1993–97, opening a window of time during which reformers were influenced by international factors. These influences were reflected in new goals for public administration reform, including an emphasis on efficiency and harmonization of provinces with those in Western Europe. This confluence of historical tradition, immediate communist past, and international influence would give rise to the ideologies, interest groups, and international pressures that influenced policy actors during the final development of county and provincial reforms.

3 A Theoretical Framework for Understanding the Politics of Decentralization

From fall, 1997, to winter, 1999, the right coalition government was engaged in numerous political battles that would ultimately compromise reform goals. During this period of intense legislative work many conflicting interests emerged, which resulted in compromises that pushed reform in unintended directions. Ideologies and pressures on policy actors stemming from a variety of historical, institutional, political, and international sources were the basis for interest coalitions formed by politicians that often cut across party affiliation. Friction between these coalitions forced politicians to compromise the original goals of reform authors. In particular, tension between ideologies of neoliberalism and neotraditionalism found in the coalition government in the area of fiscal decentralization proved to be the largest stumbling block for reform. These processes resulted in many unintended consequences and unmet goals.

Overview of the Politics of Reform

Political debates during reform development in the 1997–99 period centered around the four different aspects of public administration reform in Poland: administrative, political, and fiscal decentralization and territorial division of the state. While there is some overlap in definitions of the types of decentralization, these categories highlight separate processes that are significant when discussing development of the reform. Administrative decentralization is the redistribution of public responsibilities to lower levels of government. Political decentralization is the extension of citizen power in public decision making. Fiscal decentralization is the transfer of funds or legal instruments for raising funds to lower levels of governments along with the authority to make decisions regarding how those funds are used.[1] The territorial division of the state is the establishment of the number, size, and placement of subnational government and administrative units. Analysis of the politics of the 1999 reform addresses each of these four parts of the reform separately and shows that large-scale outcomes for each area were often influenced by the politics of more than one of these areas.

Pressures on the four aspects of the reform that resulted in compromised outcomes can be traced back to historical and contemporary sources. Historical influences that shaped the reform were found in neotraditional ideologies with roots in the precommunist system as well as in communist legacies of institutions resistant to change. For example, with the territorial division of the state, reform initiators in parliament and government espoused neotraditional ideologies calling for the return of the county system along precommunist lines within certain limits. Constituents, however, took neotraditionalism to its extreme by advocating for the return of many historical counties that went against advised guidelines for efficient administrative divisions. Thus, such action resulted in policy that undermined other goals of the reform. Similarly, in the case of administrative decentralization, those opposed to reform due to ties with the communist public administration system—namely central bureaucracies and old provincial capitals—pressured politicians to limit proposed reforms, which also resulted in policy that did not fully achieve reform goals. Haggard and Webb describe such power politics and its consequences on policy: "Politicians respond to constituent pressures because they seek to remain in office, and they exchange policy distortions for political support. The fate of any reform effort thus hinges on the political balance of power between the winners and losers of the reform effort."[2]

There were also influences on the reform that were contemporary in nature and independent of constituent pressure. These mainly involved international sources of influence, which supported neotraditional ideas of decentralization and which, in particular, had a large impact on political decentralization, especially on the type of subnational government established in provinces. Western sources were also behind neoliberal tendencies that ultimately compromised reform in the area of fiscal decentralization. As will be shown, neoliberal ideas were behind exclusionary manipulations on the part of the Ministry of Finance that left out other reform actors. Political actors being pushed and pulled in these various directions worked for or against the reform in a democratic context characterized by a presidential-parliamentary system, a balanced dual executive, and proportional representation in the lower house.

Political Theory and Postcommunist Politics

Political theory currently being used to understand postcommunist politics, with some exceptions, is roughly divided between those drawing on a rational choice perspective and those using a new institutionalist approach with an emphasis on path dependency.[3] There is also a third camp—mainly political economists—who resist the idea that political theory based on consolidated democracies can be used to explain political processes in transitioning countries.[4] Scholars drawing on new institutionalism focus on path dependency created by historical legacies and structures and ideologies in place before policy formation.[5] Others using rational or public choice approaches examine the rational choices of actors working within institutions to explain policy outcomes.[6] Some scholars have begun to analyze postcommunist policies from both new institutionalist and rational choice perspectives. For example, Cain and Surdej evaluate stalled pension reforms in Poland using transitional politics (along the lines of historical institutionalism) and public choice. They state, "Our analysis of pension policy not only illustrates the importance of history and ideas on policy developments in Poland but more precisely shows how the mechanisms of democratic functioning manipulate this history and ideas."[7]

Prior attempts at building a theoretical framework for understanding the politics of decentralization in East Central Europe have focused on the identification of various explanatory concepts or main variables of change including historical legacies (precommunist, communist, and sometimes postcommunist), ideas or ideology, institutions, and geographic considerations.[8] The emphasis of these accounts on institutions and historical and ideological influences places them in the sphere of new institutionalism. Their main weakness lies in limited analysis of the "back kitchen of politics" where the deals and compromises are made that shape final policy outcomes.

The Theory of Disjointed Pluralism

In this study, the determinants and outcomes of the second round of decentralization in Poland were best explained by drawing on the combination of rational choice and historical institutionalism found in disjointed pluralism. Though a western-based political theory, it proved to work well in a situation of postcommunist politics and was able to account for much of the political process and policy outcomes. Two exceptions were that it failed to take into consideration possible variance in the institutional design of democracies (in other words, different designs produce different numbers and kinds of veto points), and it did not account for the phenomenon of exclusionary politics characteristic of transitioning democracies.[9]

Schickler's theory of disjointed pluralism borrows from both rational choice and historical institutionalist theories and shows that a combination of the two provides a more complete understanding of processes that influence policy formation. Schickler notes that rational choice contributes to the idea that the goal-driven behavior of legislative members shapes institutional outcomes whereas historical institutionalism shows that institutions are "historical composites." He tempers the linearity of path dependency often found in historical institutionalism with the goal-driven behavior of individual members. He notes that "whereas path dependence suggests that legislative institutions likely will, in the long run, move toward a single organizational model, members' multiple goals have precluded such an outcome." The result of combining these two processes suggests the creation of institutions that are unstable and even contradictory, rather than stable institutions as much of the rational choice literature suggests. Schickler argues that "Congressional development does not produce some stable, effective compromise that is reasonably satisfactory for all (or even most) members. Instead, it produces a set of institutions that often work at cross-purposes."[10]

The theory of disjointed pluralism provides a framework that helps explain how the politics of the 1999 administrative reform led to unintended consequences. In turn, such analysis of the 1999 reform provides added support for the theory of disjointed pluralism and demonstrates the theory is applicable to institutions beyond legislative ones. In addition, it shows the theory can be applied in different democratic contexts. Rather than evaluate institutional change across four different time periods, as Schickler does, this analysis looks at the four differing but related types of institutional change (identified above) found within the same reform package. These four cases demonstrate three claims made by the theory of disjointed pluralism.[11]

The first claim is that "multiple collective interests typically shape each important change in congressional institutions."[12] This claim posits that, with a few exceptions, the political process by which institutional change occurs is not characterized by just one collective interest but by multiple interests promoted by different coalitions. The interaction between these coalitions determines the outcomes of institutional change. As Schickler states, "The 'unintended effects' of an institutional innovation often derive not from the failure of members seeking a single goal to anticipate the consequences of their actions, but rather from the tensions among the *multiple interests* that produced the change in question."[13]

Schickler identifies two ways in which this phenomenon can take place. The "common carrier" model posits that different interests may support a particular change but for different reasons—each looks to different consequences of reform that are not completely compatible.[14] In this analysis, the case of political decentralization on the provincial level provides an example of this, where potentially resistant central bureaucrats supported provincial self-government because it would facilitate EU structural funds while the main reasons for support espoused by decentralization reformers included gains to democracy and efficiency as well as EU structural funds.

The second way multiple interests can create unintended effects, and more common to this study, is a situation where change intended to fulfill a specific goal of a single interest may be compromised by concessions to other interests. This phenomenon is best expressed by Schickler: "Although those initiating a change may have a single, clear goal in mind, they often are forced to make concessions to opponents of this goal, or to members who are not hostile to the basic purpose of the reform but nonetheless believe it might adversely affect some other interest. One cannot equate the initiators' goals with the final outcome of these compromises."[15] Examples of this type of compromise are found where reformers conceded to a large number of counties to gain support for the reform as a whole. They also allowed for a substantial number of cities with county status in exchange for a reduction in the number of provinces.

Also important is Schickler's observation that a change in one aspect of a reform proposal may affect other aspects of the proposal in significant ways. The Polish reform demonstrates that this not only happened within one of the four parts but between the four parts of the broader reform proposal as well. For example, a change in one element of the plan for administrative decentralization not only affected other elements within that plan but also aspects of political and fiscal decentralization. This phenomenon is clearly demonstrated in chapter 4.

Schickler's second claim is that "entrepreneurial members build support for reform by framing proposals that appeal to groups motivated by different interests."[16] This claim further elaborates the common carrier model by positing that reform initiators establish a basis for cooperation among opposing legislators by defining proposals in a way that appeals to their interests. This was the case in the common carrier situation cited above with respect to political decentralization in the provinces. Reform initiators positively framed the proposal for provincial self-government as beneficial to initially resistant politicians by showing it would facilitate EU structural funds.

The third claim is that "congressional institutions typically develop through an accumulation of innovations that are inspired by competing motives, which engenders a tense layering of new arrangements on top of preexisting structures."[17] This claim has its roots in the path dependency model where choices open to policy makers today are dependent on previously made choices. In this case, institutions created by past decisions develop constituencies interested in preservation of power afforded that institution.[18] Schickler posits that this constrains reformers to add on new institutions rather than abolish old ones. The case of administrative decentralization in the area of provincial reforms provides an example of this where central bureaucrats were resistant to dismantling provincial offices under central government auspices. In partial response to this, a new provincial self-government was added alongside, rather than in place of, these provincial offices though few provincial functions and funds were actually transferred to the new entity. Similarly, central government ministries generally strove and at times succeeded in preventing the decentralization of tasks to lower levels of government, even though subnational institutions had been created to undertake them.

Veto Points in the Polish Political System

Overlooked by Schickler's analysis is the role a country's specific democratic framework can have in structuring the power and behavior of reform actors. The Polish political system is particularly susceptible to veto points that create opportunities for the involvement of other reform actors. Veto points or gates are "institutions with the power to influence or block policy initiatives."[19] Multiple veto points let in a wide array of interests, which necessitates the negotiations and compromises of disjointed pluralism. Thus, the type of political system, in terms of its veto points, structures the number and kinds of compromises outlined in disjointed pluralism.

The number of veto points can have the power to affect the course of policymaking. In general, multiple veto points can limit the government's ability to control policy outcomes, while the absence of veto points concentrates power in the hands of the government, increasing its ability to pass its policy measures. Compromise necessitated by veto points may broaden political support for reform but at the expense of reform objectives, which may be diluted in the process. Moreover, the number and type of veto points shape the pattern of power distribution in a political system, which can affect reformers' strategies for policymaking.[20]

Poland has a presidential-parliamentary political system defined by a dual executive, bicameralism, and proportional representation. These characteristics resulted in veto points that gave the government relatively limited control over parliament during development of the 1999 reform. Negotiation and compromise resulted in the eventual passage of reforms through these veto points in the areas of administrative and political decentralization and the territorial division of the state. However, compromises that facilitated the passage of reforms resulted in unintended consequences and undermined some original goals of the reform.

Poland's mixed presidential-parliamentary system provides the government with less control over parliament than in strictly parliamentary systems though slightly more control than in a separation-of-powers arrangement.[21] In Poland's political system, as in a separation-of-powers system, a divided government can occur when the president and the parliamentary group in power are from different parties.[22] This was the situation during development of the administrative reforms because President Aleksander Kwaśniewski, a former communist and member of the Democratic Left Alliance, held office at the same time that the Solidarity Electoral Action (AWS) and Freedom Union (UW) coalition was in power in parliament and controlled key ministerial posts. This arrangement created a veto point that President Kwaśniewski took advantage of by literally vetoing parliament's first bill on the number of provinces, forcing further compromise on AWS's first proposal for provinces. In the Polish system, this veto point overlaps with another identified veto point, that of a balanced dual executive.[23] At the time of reform development, President Kwaśniewski shared executive power with Prime Minister Jerzy Buzek of AWS.

Poland's government also has less control over parliamentary decisions because the government, in terms of the prime minister and the Council of Ministers, does not have the power to dissolve parliament and call for new elections (the president has this power but only in limited situations outlined in the Constitution). This means the parliament can act against government proposals without fear of being dissolved. It also opens a door for interest groups to pressure members of parliament in directions that are not in line with government proposals.[24] With the 1999 reforms, interest groups had considerable influence on the outcome of the territorial division of the state (the final number of counties and provinces) and some influence on outcomes for administrative decentralization.

An important way the Polish political system does allow government to exert pressure on parliament is through the government's power to dissolve itself. Parliaments that have a significant say in the formation of a government most likely have a stake in its continuance. A government in this position is therefore able to keep parliament in line with the threat of dissolving itself.[25] It appears, however, that the Polish government never outwardly used this threat during development of the 1999 reform, perhaps because the government itself was often split on reform issues and unable to present a unified voice.

Bicameralism and proportional representation are also potential veto points in the Polish political system. Bicameralism can act as a veto point when the two chambers of parliament are elected according to different electoral laws, making it possible for the two chambers to have different party compositions.[26] In Poland, the Sejm is elected according to proportional representation while the Senate is elected according to majority vote, a situation that may result in dissimilar party compositions in the two chambers. During the 1997–2001 legislative term, however, the AWS-UW coalition held a majority in both the Sejm and the Senate. Thus, the situation did not trigger bicameralism as a veto point.

Proportional representation acts as a veto point when it results in many small parties and coalitions of parties. Governments established by coalitions produce more veto opportunities because disagreements between coalition partners may create more conflict than would be the case in single-party governments, especially if one partner is promoting unpopular legislation.[27] Moreover, Haggard and Webb note, "Fragmentation [tendency toward the proliferation of political parties] makes coalition rule more likely, increases the difficulty of reaching compromises, and contributes to the instability of governments—all factors that can effect government policy."[28]

Proportional representation and party fragmentation in the Polish Sejm were factors in the creation of both the AWS and the AWS-UW coalition. The AWS was itself a coalition of over thirty moderate and center-right parties and organizations under the leadership of the Solidarity Trade Union. Three main strands within AWS often came in tension with one another: the Solidarity trade unionists, the liberal-conservatives of the Conservative-Peasant Party (SKL), and the Christian nationalists of the Christian National Union (ZChN). AWS was especially divided in the area of economic policy.[29] The creation of the AWS-UW coalition after the 1997 elections highlighted this rift in AWS as UW was decidedly pro-market. To complicate matters further, Leszek Balcerowicz, famous for the shock therapy reforms of the early 1990s, simultaneously headed up both the UW and the Ministry of Finance. Differences on fiscal decentralization between AWS (and some UW) members of parliament and the neoliberal Ministry of Finance were significant factors behind stalled fiscal decentralization. At times, stalemates between the two could only be resolved with the intervention of Prime Minister Jerzy Buzek (AWS).[30]

Policymaking in a Transitioning Country

Division within the AWS-UW coalition was not the only factor behind problems with fiscal policy for the 1999 reform. The neoliberal approach to policymaking favors the use of exclusionary politics during reform development. Greskovits, in his study of reform in East Central Europe, finds that a "characteristic of the neoliberal reform process is its secrecy and failure to consult with other bureaucratic and political actors."[31] In Poland, creation of fiscal policy for the reform was de facto centralized to one neoliberal decision-maker who, in various ways, strove to bypass or disengage other policy actors through isolation and misinformation. As a consequence, his policy suggestions lacked the support of the government and parliament. This situation was in part responsible for two failed attempts at the passage of fiscal decentralization legislation (in 1998 and 2000) and the underfunding of services after decentralization and ultimately compromised goals in the areas of democracy and improved public services. Haggard and Kaufman state, "Centralized decision making reduces the scope of policy advice the government receives and reduces the incentives for consensus building, consultation, and feedback, which may be essential to the sustainability (if not the initiation) of the reform effort."[32] The situation was compounded by the distributive nature of fiscal decentralization reforms. As Haggard and Kaufman also note, "The advantages of centralized decision making decrease and the importance of representation increases in reforms characterized by strong distributive conflicts."[33]

The reforms were also characterized by the limitations of Polish policymakers themselves. Cognitive limitations and inexperience of policymakers as well as the short time they gave themselves to push reforms through were all factors shaping the reform development environment. Schickler argues that "the limited cognitive capacities of decision makers, who must evaluate the complex implications of proposed institutions" contributes to solutions that are not always optimal.[34] Add to this the particular transition environment found in postcommunist politics, and the chances for good policymaking are limited even further. On politics in East Central Europe scholars note that "overloaded policymakers attempt[ed] to develop responses to the fast-paced and complex problems of transition in a world of uncertainty."[35]

4 The Politics of Decentralization, 1997–98

From fall, 1997, through 1998 members of parliament, government officials, bureaucrats, researchers, interest groups, and average citizens weighed in on discussions about public administration reform in an effort to influence written reform policy. Sub-debates sprang up around each of the four parts of the reform: administrative, political, and fiscal decentralization, and territorial division of the state. Each sub-debate attracted a different group of opponents that reformers had to contend with. Reform initiators were often politicians with local self-government experience who had come to parliament for the express purpose of pushing through public administration reforms. These so-called "self-government" politicians ("self-governmenters") had a strong presence in the right coalition government but were also found among social democrats on the left. Their reform proposals were influenced by neoliberal ideas, interest groups, and international factors.

Administrative Decentralization

The sub-debate on administrative decentralization took place mainly between "self-government" politicians and government officials on the one hand and central ministry bureaucrats and trade unions on the other.[1] In this sub-debate "self-government" politicians and government officials in charge of the reform were driven primarily by three factors: a neotraditional ideology calling for a return to the state of affairs before communism, Western views of decentralization espoused by the Council of Europe and the European Union (EU), and a political interest in putting "communist" bureaucratic institutions under local control. The first two influences on administrative decentralization, neotraditionalism and a Western view of decentralization, were also instrumental in reformers' thinking on political and fiscal decentralization addressed later. Those resisting specifically administrative decentralization were central ministry bureaucrats concerned with maintaining control over government responsibilities to retain power over jobs and funds. Also, some

Table 1. Laws of Poland's 1999 Public Administration Reform

Administrative Decentralization	
The Competence Law	Law of July 24, 1998, on the change of some laws defining the competencies of public administration organs—in association with the state systemic reform. (Dz.U. Nr 106, poz. 668)
Implementation Law for Administrative Reforms	Law of October 13, 1998—Regulations implementing laws reforming the public administration. (Dz.U. Nr 133, poz. 872)
Political Decentralization	
Law on County Self-Government	Law of June 5, 1998, on county self-government. (Dz.U. Nr 91, poz. 578)
Law on Provincial Self-Government	Law of June 5, 1998, on the self-government of the province. (Dz.U. Nr 91, poz. 576)
Law on Central Government Administration in the Province	Law of June 5, 1998, on governmental administration in the province. (Dz.U. Nr 91, poz. 577)
Electoral Law for Subnational Governments	Law of June 16, 1998—Electoral law for municipal councils, county councils, and provincial parliaments. (Dz.U. Nr 95, poz. 602)
Implementation Law for New Subnational Governments	Law of July 24, 1998, on the starting dates of the law on county self-government, law on self-government of the province, and the law on governmental administration in the province. (Dz.U. Nr 99, poz. 631)
Territorial Division of the State	
Law on Territorial Division of the State	Law of July 24, 1998, on the introduction of the basic three-tier territorial division of the state. (Dz.U. Nr 96, poz. 603 sprost. Nr 104, poz 656)
Decree on the Formation of Counties	Decree of the Council of Ministers from August 7, 1998, on the matter of the formation of counties. (Dz.U. Nr 103, poz. 652)
Fiscal Decentralization	
Law on Public Finance	Law of November 26, 1998, on public finance. (Dz.U. Nr 155, poz. 1014)
Revenue Law for Subnational Governments	Law of November 26, 1998, on revenues of territorial self-government entities in the years 1999 and 2000. (Dz.U. Nr 150, poz. 983)

Sources: Chancellory of the Prime Minister, *Effectiveness, Openness, Subsidiarity: A New Poland for New Challenges;* B. Czubaszek, ed., *Ustrój Administracji Przepisów: Zbiór Najnowszych Przepisów;* Dorota Kutyla, ed., *Zasadniczy Trójstopniowy Podział Terytorialny Polski: Komentarz do Przepisów.*

Note: Each entry on the right includes the formal name of the law translated into English by the author and its reference number (in parentheses) for the Polish Journal of Laws.

trade unions resisted administrative decentralization because it would mean loss of influence over issues currently controlled in the center and thus also loss of bargaining power with the central government.

Ideologies

Neotraditionalism supported certain theoretical arguments about the benefits of administrative and political decentralization. These mainly centered on improvements in efficiency and civil society and the reduction of corruption. Deficiencies in these areas were attributed to the centralized system put in place by communists.

Table 2. Summary of the Sub-debates of the 1999 Public Administration Reform

	Main Actors	Main Influences on Actors	Reform Result
Administrative Decentralization	"self-government" politicians and officials vs. central ministries	neotraditionalism; West European views; de-communization vs. legacy of centralized bureaucracies	Central ministries have a fair amount of influence: a number of tasks set for decentralization remain centralized.
Political Decentralization: Counties	"self-government" politicians and officials vs. Polish Peasant Party	neotraditionalism; West European views; de-communization vs. perceived loss of party power in rural areas	Self-government politicians monopolize the debate: counties are established as self-governing units.
Political Decentralization: Provinces	Institute of Public Affairs vs. the Catholic right and some left centralists	West European provincial government; some neotraditionalism vs. memory of a partitioned Poland; legacy of centralization	Institute of Public Affairs proves influential with its arguments: provinces are established with a central government presence *and* a self-governing body.
Territorial Division of the State: Counties	"self-government" politicians and officials vs. Ministry of Finance	neotraditionalism; pressure from local groups for many, old counties vs. calculated inefficiency of many, small counties	"Self-government" politicians listen to their local constituents: many, small counties are created.
Territorial Division of the State: Provinces	right coalition government officials; Institute of Public Affairs vs. left coalition and some right coalition politicians	neotraditionalism; West European example; European Union and Council of Europe vs. pressure from local groups to not abolish certain provincial capitals	The left coalition and president overpower a divided right coalition: four more provinces are added to the right's original list of twelve.
Fiscal Decentralization	"self-government" politicians and officials vs. Ministry of Finance	neotraditionalism; European Union; Council of Europe vs. neoliberalism	Disagreement stalls discussion on fiscal decentralization: no reform is passed. Ministry of Finance appears to surreptitiously underfund decentralized tasks.

Efficiency, reformers believed, would be improved in two ways: through restructuring the public administration system, including the administration in the center, and through increased rationality in public expenditures. Rationality was expected to increase as subnational units, in a better position to identify where waste occurs, would redirect funds to where they were needed most. Decentralization was also believed to strengthen civil society through the addition of new self-governments on the provincial and county levels and was thought to reduce corruption through increased transparency of public finances. The connection between democracy on subnational levels and improvement in public services was a strong argument of reformers. Michał Kulesza, the government plenipotentiary for the reform, stated that with the reform there "begins to function in practice a citizen state in which democratic factors work on behalf of improving the institutional conditions of collective life."[2] So strongly held were these beliefs in the theoretical benefits of the reform that Kulesza stated, "Putting off the reform again would not only carry measurable losses for civilization but also for the economic development of the country and direct financial damage."[3]

International Influence

Reform initiators were also influenced in their approach to decentralization by Western European thought and example surrounding the idea of subsidiarity. For example, the Council of Europe outwardly calls for subsidiarity in its Charter on Local Government. It also states, "Local government denotes the right and the ability of local authorities ... to regulate and manage a substantial share of public affairs under their own responsibility and in the interests of the local population."[4] (See appendix B for relevant excerpts from the Charter on Local Government.) A similar emphasis on subsidiarity is found in the Draft Charter on Regional Self-Government. Poland has agreed to both charters, which directly prompted reformers to push for reforms in the area of administrative decentralization.[5]

The EU also supports the idea of subsidiarity in a general sense, but different EU countries interpret it differently. Best notes, "In most of continental Europe, subsidiarity is the essence of federalism. In the UK, in particular, it is used simply to mean a 'default' preference against doing things at the Community (EU) level."[6] The general principle as stated in article A of the Common Provisions in the Treaty of Maastricht is that the Union should be one "in which decisions are taken as closely as possible to the citizen," reflecting wording also found in the Treaty's preamble. The legal parameters of this statement, however, extend only to decisions regarding what action should be taken at the EU level, as clarified by article 3b of the Treaty Establishing the European Community.[7] Poland, nonetheless, apparently is among those countries to have taken a broad interpretation of the EU statement on subsidiarity. One reformer said that "The decentralization of state tasks through the development of territorial self-government has for several years been an organizational priority of European Union countries. This results from the Treaty of Maastricht that commands application of the principle of subsidiarity (pomocniczość) by European Union member countries and from the need to meet citizen expectations for greater influence over public affairs."[8]

Even though in principle the EU has no basis in the Maastricht or Amsterdam treaties for intervention in matters of internal decentralization, this has not precluded informal prodding on the part of the EU in this direction.[9] Such influence is found in specific country assessments prepared by the European Union for accessioning countries. For example, in a 1998 progress report Poland's decision to establish self-governed provinces and counties was listed as one of its accomplishments.[10] Thus, Poland's broad interpretation of the EU statement on subsidiarity and the EU's indirect pressure together would imply that Poland was considerably influenced by the EU regarding administrative (and political) decentralization, even though Poland is aware that such reforms are not formally required for EU accession. Even taken together, though, the outside influence of European organizations appears to be more supportive than decisive in reformers' plans for administrative and political decentralization. That is, there was enough internal pressure for decentralization that it probably would have occurred without outside influence, although such influence no doubt helped shape and spur it on.[11]

Interest Groups

A third motivator for mainly administrative decentralization but also a new state territorial division was a political reason—to decommunize the administrative bureaucracy and put government responsibilities more directly under control of the people (though also motivated by neotraditionalism). Administrative decentralization was intended not only to decentralize many ministerial tasks but also to dismantle deconcentrated special administrations that existed on the level of newly proposed counties and were directly subordinate to the ministries. Many ministerial duties and special administrations were to be transferred to elected county and provincial governments, taking them out of the hands of old party bureaucrats and putting them under control of the people.

Given this pointed attack on the existent public administration system, it was no wonder central bureaucracies put up considerable resistance during reform development. Well-entrenched ministries were reluctant to have their responsibilities and funds decentralized to lower levels of government and fought any kind of restructuring of the administration at the center. Loss of control over ministerial tasks and deconcentrated special administrations and funds for them meant a significant loss of jobs and power for ministries. Among central ministries there was also the mentality that if an administrative task was important it should stay in the hands of the state administration and not be passed to "incompetent" locally elected officials.[12] Interestingly, ministers were in favor of decentralization in general but not when it came to their own ministry—each felt his or her ministry should be the exception. Thus, outcomes in this area differed largely according to the political influence of a given ministry and the willingness of reformers to compromise in their demands in exchange for a minister's support of the reform as a whole.[13]

The following examples provide a picture of outcomes resulting from the sub-debate between "self-government" politicians with government officials and several central ministries. The Ministry of Environmental Protection in particular fought hard to keep its special administration intact. Apparently its main motivation was to protect its political influence over the hiring of people to important positions in its field administrations, a battle it won, which resulted in continued centralization of many environmental protection programs.[14] In the reform of the national health care system (which predated the public administration reform by about a year), the Ministry of Health saw new special administrations actually added to its responsibilities. Rather than place new health care funds under the auspices of elected county government, standing funds were organized in a separate territorial arrangement and subordinated to the Ministry of Health. This centralization of the health system was not altered with the public administration reform. Lack of such administrative decentralization weakened local self-government and increased bureaucracy, providing outcomes that were the exact opposite of reform goals.[15]

On the other hand, the Ministry of Labor and Social Policy and the Ministry of Education reluctantly submitted to the decentralization of many of their responsibilities, with some exceptions. Though many social services (narrowly defined) were immediately decentralized with the reform (see chapter 5), the Ministry of Labor and Social Policy successfully held off reform of the labor system for a year after general reform implementation. Only after a fierce legislative battle in 1999 did self-government reformers place much of the administration of labor programs under county government auspices beginning in 2000.[16] A similar situation occurred with the Ministry of Education. With education the vision of reformers won out and essentially all remaining educational institutions were decentralized to new county and provincial self-government. Almost all secondary schools and primary schools for the disabled were transferred to the county level as well as many non-school educational facilities.[17] Provincial self-governments were given the responsibility for secondary schools for social workers and nurses, teacher colleges, and in-service vocational training centers. The Ministry of Education, with the help of teachers' trade unions (see below), did manage to maintain significant centralized control over the establishment of curriculum standards, teachers' qualifications and pay levels, and levels of student achievement and classification. Other ministries, however, resisted giving up vocational schools in their sectors with the result that the Ministry of Internal Affairs and Administration continues to maintain three schools for firefighters; the Ministry of Defense has two military lyceums; and the Ministry of Justice still operates thirty-four primary schools, thirty vocational schools, and twenty-four adult education facilities. Only after a year's delay and another fierce legislative battle did the Ministry of Culture finally decentralize 161 vocational art schools in 2000. Adverse outcomes in general due to compromises over administrative decentralization included internal inconsistencies and limited effectiveness of the territorial administration.[18]

Some trade unions also staunchly opposed administrative decentralization in their respective areas. Administrative decentralization for them meant that decisions on issues important to them would be made at the local level, and thus their influence over issues currently controlled in the center would be lost. Such loss of influence on the central level would also mean loss of bargaining power with the central government. Two unions, the Solidarity Labor Union and the Polish Teachers Union, were able to significantly influence the reform process in the area of decentralization though with differing degrees of impact on outcomes.[19]

The Solidarity Labor Union joined forces with the Ministry of Labor and Social Policy and the National Labor Office in order to prevent the decentralization of labor programs to lower levels of government. The labor union's main argument was that while decentralization generally speaking is a good thing, labor programs should be treated differently because of a need for flexibility in responding to unpredictable unemployment crises in different regions of the country. If labor funds were dispersed to local governments according to an established formula as a result of administrative decentralization, the central government would not have the funds to address unexpected crises in unemployment. Of equal or more concern may have also been the fact that the labor union stood to lose a considerable piece of political leverage once its centrally established influence over labor funds was dispersed along with the decentralization of tasks and corresponding transfer of funds. The Union-Ministry-Office coalition was successful enough to delay decentralization of the labor system for a year while the rest of the administrative reform went forward. During that year, however, the agenda-setting power held by staunch decentralists in parliament made it impossible for labor centralists to get revisions made in legislation set to decentralize the labor system in January, 2000. Their one victory was the maintenance on the central level of a program for unemployed recent graduates.[20]

The pressure of the Polish Teachers Union had a more significant influence on reform outcomes in the area of education. The large pressure this group placed on reformers resulted in a situation where responsibility for teachers working on subnational levels was split between local government and parliament. That is, while local government officials are the formal employers of teachers, the conditions of their employment are determined in parliament with the active participation of trade unions.[21] Here again, the fear of losing influence over reforms regarding teachers as a result of decentralization apparently prompted the union to press for the status quo. Other outcomes for administrative decentralization are connected to the lack of fiscal decentralization and the underfunding of decentralized services that impeded their adequate implementation.

Lack of state restructuring in the center was one of the main political compromises reformers made in order to gain support for the reform. But the extent and significance of the amount of decentralization that actually occurred appears to be a matter of perspective. For example, one reformer went so far as to state in 1998 (before reforms were even implemented), "In opposition to many public statements—beyond the sphere of central investment—self-governments [provincial and county] did not receive as a result of the reform any essential functions executed to this point by ministers."[22] On the other hand, Kulesza emphasized a compromise with ministries over the downsizing of ministerial jobs rather than a compromise over decentralization. He stated that a lot of ministerial duties were in fact decentralized and as a consequence many ministry workers were no longer necessary. He then admitted, "ministries should have been downsized as a part of the reform but I could not create another group of enemies if I wanted the main reforms accepted."[23] Without question, however, compromises with ministries over decentralization and downsizing were made and resulted in stalled reforms and unexpected outcomes.

Political Decentralization

A different mix of policy actors came forward when issues of political decentralization were raised. This group was divided even further as different actors formed around debates on political decentralization to county and provincial levels.

Counties

Promoters of political decentralization to the county level were the same self-government politicians and right coalition government officials pushing for administrative decentralization. As shown above, the various factors influencing reformers' thinking on administrative decentralization simultaneously supported political decentralization. Thus, here again, neotraditionalism, Western views on decentralization, and the goal of placing "communist" bureaucratic institutions under local control were all major factors influencing political decentralization to the county level. However, the ideology of neotraditionalism played the most direct and influential role.

The ideology of neotraditionalism was particularly strong in the case of county government reform. Before World War II Poland's local government structure followed a dual model of public administration whose roots can be traced back to the former

Austro-Hungarian Monarchy (1862). In this model, democratically elected local governments perform both their own tasks and tasks delegated to them from the state administration.[24] This form of local government was restored to the municipal level with the 1990 *Law on Local Self-Government* and self-government politicians and government officials sought to restore it to counties with the 1998 reform.

The only opposition to county self-government came in the form of the Polish Peasant Party (PSL) and a group of expert scholars from the Center for Self-Government and Local Development at the University of Warsaw, whose project was endorsed by the PSL. As explained earlier, the PSL was against county reforms because it was afraid its party's power would be undermined by new counties diluting the political influence of rural municipalities.[25]

Expert scholars from the center prepared a project based loosely on local government in France that provided an alternative model to self-governed counties. Their main idea was that to be truly created in a democratic fashion from the bottom up, supra-municipal local governments should be created by existing municipalities as they identified need for them. Groups of municipalities would come together in municipal associations to take care of those services best provided on a slightly higher level of government. The existing forty-nine counties and the forty-six large cities that were already cooperating in the County Pilot Project would be established as counties (above the associations) with a dozen or so newly created provinces above that. The counties would be governed by a representative of the central government, not locally elected officials, thus ensuring a true unitary state.[26]

The PSL latched on to this project because it largely maintained the existing order of things and thereby ensured the continuance of their power. In addition, retention of the forty-nine provinces, though now called counties, would make it possible for many of their party members working in the provincial administration to continue in their positions. Efforts to get the project on the parliamentary floor, however, were in vain. Even the parliamentary committee on local government and regional policy allowed only one presentation of the project and dismissed any further attempts for its discussion. Moreover, the center invited right reformers to its conferences and seminars for an open discussion of the reform but none ever came—only those from the left participated (including many from SLD).[27] Clearly, though, as far as political decentralization for counties, the center's project completely undermined reformers' goals in this area as it would have for the territorial division of the state as well. There was thus an early embargo of the PSL project, and the general consensus among remaining policy actors resulted in a system of county self-government, which was, however, to be relatively weak.

Outcomes in the area of political decentralization show that counties did not get a chance to exercise their powers of self-government to the extent expected due to compromises on administrative decentralization as discussed in the section on administrative decentralization above and lack of fiscal decentralization (see section on fiscal decentralization in this chapter).

Provinces

The extent of political decentralization to the provincial level was established by the right-leaning Institute of Public Affairs, whose policy actors convinced those initially opposed to their plan, the Catholic right and some left centralists, of its necessity to facilitate EU structural funds early on in the game. Thus, the story of the type of provincial government lies largely in an explanation of influences on policy actors within the institute itself. The institute was started in 1994 by a prominent official of the first right government and expert scholars from various universities. It was funded by Western (mostly United States) sources and had as its goal the preparation of legislation for when the government was once again in the hands of the right.[28] (The left government, though slow in starting, did some work on the regional reforms during this time in conjunction with a task force they established with the Council of Europe, but it only resulted in recommendations, not legislation.[29]) One of the projects of the institute was the preparation of legislation on the type of government to be established in the provinces. Neotraditionalism and Western European influences shaped plans that resulted in a dual system of provincial government: provincial self-government and a provincial arm of the central government operating entirely separate from one another. Here neotraditionalism appeared to play a minimal role that was enough to keep a central government presence on the provincial level but not enough to prevent the establishment of provincial self-government. As will be shown, Western influences were the decisive factors in the creation of provincial self-government, an act that went against historical precedence and to some extent societal wishes. A brief history of regional government in Poland and earlier attempts at regional government reform set the stage to show how Western influences in the end dominated over an established traditional model.

During the interwar years Polish provinces were governed by regional agencies of the central government inspired by the French prefecturial model. This system continued under communism with provincial government still being subordinated to central government administration. After the fall of communism, the first time a serious proposal for regionalization was made was under the Bielecki government in 1990–91. Plans called for the creation of regions with two-house representation equipped with legislative competencies, as well as a regional central government presence. This regional structure was based on the German *Länder* model and thus was tied to a federalist system. This proposal, however, met with much resistance because Poles were not ready for regional self-government, especially one patterned after the German model. Memories of a strong, dominant Germany were bolstered at the time by the unification of East and West Germany, and fears of the return of a strong Germany were widespread in Polish society. Poles saw the creation of Polish "*Länder*" as the first step towards restructuring Poland along German lines, leading eventually to loss of Polish sovereignty so recently regained.[30] Poles also had a historical memory of a partitioned Poland, which fed fears that strong regions may eventually demand their own autonomy and lead to the break-up of Poland.[31] Such pressures undermined this first proposal for regionalization and ensured that Poland would remain a unitary and not a federalist state. Indeed, reform working groups under the Bielecki government changed their focus to the creation of ten to twelve large provinces overseen by central government administration only. Work on provincial reforms moved forward again under the Suchocka government from July, 1992, to September, 1993. Plans for twelve, seventeen, and twenty-five provinces were drawn up as well as a plan for continued central government administration in the provinces. An early legislative project on provincial self-government had been thrown out by parliament in its first reading in January, 1993, with the official reasoning that self-government needed to be built from the bottom up, county self-government being next in line.[32]

Reformers at the Institute of Public Affairs picked up the work on provincial reforms in 1994. Their legislative project, the *Law on Self-government and Central Government Administration in the Province,* was formally presented in the summer of 1997 a few months before the right came to power again.[33] Despite clear societal resistance to provincial self-government and lack of a historical model for it, the project called for the establishment of both a self-governing provincial government and a separate central government administration on the provincial level. The following discussion showing Western influences on the reform is based on an Institute for Public Affairs report published in August, 1997, that introduced the legislative project. In the report specific consideration was taken of the European Parliament's *Community Charter on Regionalization,* the European Union's policy requirements for structural funds, the Council of Europe's *European Charter on Regional Self-Government,* and the examples of Western European countries and their regions that operate under these supra-national institutions.

The advisory *Community Charter on Regionalization,* adopted by the European Parliament in 1988, outlines a division of tasks in the state structure between central authority and regional self-government. It stipulates, among other things, that principle traits of a region should include financial independence and the right to cooperation in decisions undertaken by the nation and European communities. Of particular confusion for reformers was the kind of regional model the contents of the charter were calling for—self-government as in France or the politically autonomous regions of Italy or Spain. The Institute of Public Affairs report states, "The statements of this document are sufficiently general that it is not possible to extract a concrete answer from them. It must have had to be this way given the fact that different states had to accept it."[34] Faced with this dilemma, reformers turned to the goals the European Union established for regions. The same report continues, "For the essence of the region one must rather look through the prism of goals the European Union establishes for itself in this area (strengthening the cultural unity of regions, respecting regional distinctiveness, respecting regional aspirations, expanding the sphere of citizen responsibility). The most appropriate region model in a given country is the one that realizes most fully the above called-for goals."[35]

In general, the European Union's comments on regional administration directed at East-Central European countries indicate a preference for democratic regional self-governments with significant financial and legal autonomy.[36] The EU was clearly influential in its indirect incentive for the creation of a regional government system that would meet the EU's requirements for disbursement of structural funds. In addition, reformers believed that meeting these provisions would allow them to compete on the same level as other EU regions for such funds. While aware that the European Union does not require member states to unify administrative structures, reformers saw that a specific regional arrangement does result from spatial-economic prerequisites. These "effectively encourage states to a kind of shaping of internal structures so that specific regions can conduct independent economic politics making possible effective competition over accessible structural funds." In considering regional reforms in their own country, Polish reformers noted that "a condition for use of structural funds (and not only, because this rule is universally applied in the Union) is the proper preparation of Polish institutional infrastructure for the acceptance and use of community [EU] assistance." Reformers identified as particularly necessary the creation of independent regional public authorities that could develop and execute development programs and participate in the shaping and supervising of established programs. The report placed an emphasis on structural funds for Poland, noting at the conclusion of a section on the funds that they address the sore points of Poland's economic transformation and "how useful it would be to use resources from these funds."[37]

Though work on the Council of Europe's *European Charter on Regional Self-Government* was underway at the same time as work on Polish provincial reforms, that charter was also a factor leading to regional self-government in Poland. It establishes the right of regional inhabitants to participate in decision-making in their own affairs and regional possession of its own tasks and competencies as shaped by the principle of subsidiarity. It also calls for direct elections to a legislative organ, the independence of separate subnational governments from one another, and financial independence for the region, among other things.[38]

Reformers also looked to the experience of Western European countries deemed comparable to Poland in terms of type of government (unitary), size and population, economic and cultural potential, and movement in the direction of decentralization. Reformers chose three countries—France, Spain, and Italy—and used their experiences in designing a provincial government system for Poland. These countries' experiences were most influential in reinforcing the idea of a self-governing body in the provinces and in providing a solution for how unitary states can simultaneously maintain a central government presence on the provincial level. The solution employed by each of these three countries is the presence of two completely separate public authorities on the provincial level; that is, the establishment of both a regional self-government and a central government representative on this level. Spain and Italy's success with separate administrations for each of these entities (compared to France's difficulties with one administration serving both) was also an underlying factor in the creation of two administrations for Poland.[39]

As demonstrated, international factors were very influential in determining the system of provincial government, especially when considering the lack of historical precedence and general lack of societal support for regional self-government in Poland going into the last phase of provincial reform development in 1994. Experts who prepared the reform, especially Jan Maria Rokita, were successful in convincing both left and right members of parliament of the necessity of instituting their proposal for provincial government and their legislative project became law with some few changes.[40]

Observation of the outcomes for political decentralization to the provincial level reveals that resistance to provincial self-government resurfaced later when the AWS conservative right attempted to limit the actual transfer of power from central ministries to provincial self-governments. The debate, which was actually played out between the conservatives, centrists, and liberals of the right coalition, resulted in provincial self-governments being given a large share of responsibility for regional development but with few funds for implementation.[41] Thus, though the instrument for political power was passed to provincial self-governments, lack of funds limited the extent to which they could actually realize that power. Pressure to maintain certain responsibilities under the auspices of provincial central government also led to negative outcomes. The structural law, which laid the foundation for the new administrative system, established the responsibilities of each of the provincial governments in broad terms. However, the realization of that law in terms of specific legislation on the division of competencies left more responsibilities in the hands of the provincial central government administration than reformers expected, leaving this specific legislation in conflict with the broader law. The result was not only limited provincial self-government but also an on-going competition between the two provincial governments for authority over different competencies.[42]

Administrative and political decentralization at times led to consequences that actors on both sides of these sub-debates did not predict. One of the most serious was an exacerbation of corruption with implementation of the reform. According to a 1999 Polish public opinion survey, 39 percent of respondents believed that corruption was prevalent in subnational government administration.[43] A World Bank study conducted in 1999 also highlighted corruption in Polish subnational government. It warned that the risk of corruption is greater where authority for an area overlaps between municipal, county, and provincial governments because transparency in lines of responsibility is reduced.[44] Indeed, authors of an overview of corruption in Poland stated, "There is widespread agreement that corruption is a major problem in local government, especially after Poland's extensive decentralizing reforms."[45]

Territorial Division of the State

Reforms to the territorial division of the state involved deciding the exact number and size of counties and provinces. Here again different actors were involved in the debates over counties and provinces.

Counties

With the reform for county divisions, self-government politicians and government officials were at odds with the Ministry of Finance. Officials in the ministry had determined the greatest amount of administrative efficiency could be achieved with about half the number of counties presented by the government.[46] Here, neotraditionalism and politics of self-government politicians and government officials held sway over Ministry of Finance arguments based on the effectiveness and efficiency of new county units.

The neotraditionalism of self-government politicians and government officials stemmed from the fact that the existence of three hundred counties had long been a part of Polish territorial history. Counties had been in existence in Poland from before the partitioning of the country in 1795 until 1975 when they were abolished by the communist party. Reformers thus felt compelled to restore Poland's territorial structure to its pre-war, precommunist state—to undo what had been forced upon them. Restoration of the county level in particular was viewed as a step in the direction of returning Poland to its rightful democratic structure.[47] Counties were viewed as "small fatherlands" (*małe ojczyzny*) with their own cultural identities that deserved the right to self-government almost as much as Poland as a country deserved this right.[48] Reformers additionally held that the three hundred or so capital cities of these former counties formed traditional, local centers of community and economic life; these, it was claimed, were needed for revitalization of Polish provincial regions.[49] This pre-socialist legacy so strongly shaped reformers' ideology regarding county reforms that in the end it prevailed over other ideologies for the reform.

In order to assure that county lines were drawn according to existing local identity and historical memory of citizens, reformers sent surveys to municipalities asking them to decide which counties they wanted to belong to. They were asked to adhere to a 5-10-50 formula: each county was to have a minimum of five municipalities, at least ten thousand inhabitants in the county capital, and a population of at least fifty thousand. In addition, the parliamentary committee on self-government and regional policy went to great lengths to hear hundreds of delegations that came to Warsaw on behalf of citizens of potential counties.[50]

Another factor shaping the county reform was a legacy stemming from the socialist period when counties were recipients of funding from Warsaw (counties were in existence under socialism until 1975). Due to this legacy, old county regions believed that the existence of a county was a way to tap into central government funds despite the fact that fiscal decentralization was planned and new counties were intended to be as autonomous as possible.[51] All of these factors worked to drive the number of counties higher and higher.

This explanation for outputs of the county reform would appear to be sufficient if it were not for the fact that such a large number of counties were deemed administratively inefficient and harmful to county democracy. The Ministry of Finance, guided by an ideology of efficiency and not one of historical cultural identity, proposed a project of 150 economically effective counties. It presented a list of counties that should not be created because they would undermine the efficiency of the administrative system and were too small to have the required degree of economic self-sufficiency. This last point should have been of particular concern to all reformers because economic self-sufficiency is generally seen as a prerequisite for the autonomous democratic functioning of subnational levels, a main goal of the reform. Moreover, Kulesza allowed for the creation of seventy-one counties (almost one quarter of all new counties) that did not fulfill one of the three criteria he originally formulated.[52]

Politics explains how in the end the number of counties leapt dramatically beyond the Ministry of Finance's and even reformers' rational limits. The government knew that parliamentary members were eager to establish counties in their districts because of the local clamor for them and used this knowledge to manipulate support for other areas of the reform. A paraphrased excerpt from an interview with a member of parliament describes what this situation led to: "There are also too many counties because we succumbed to political blackmail so representatives would support the reform. We bought representatives. If a representative was not in favor of the reform—was going to vote against it—we gave them a county in their region in exchange for their vote. Representatives would say they would not vote in favor of the reform unless they were given a county in their region.... It was a compromise—a worse solution for the reform in exchange for the reform to happen at all. It was the price we had to pay to have the reform."[53]

Also tied to the county reform was a political compromise necessitated by another socialist legacy—the existence of forty-nine small provinces created in 1975 by the communist party. Reformers had plans to drastically reduce the number of provinces (see discussion on provincial territorial reform in this chapter). Capital cities of proposed liquidated provinces in particular resisted the reform because they would lose their status as provincial capitals. This group carried significant weight in parliament and threatened to stall the administrative reform. Thus, as another compromise of the reform, cities were offered the status of both a municipality and a county (referred to as cities with county status) in exchange for their support of the reform. The same member of parliament noted, "We also knew that allowing the creation of cities with county status was not sensible. Here again we succumbed to political blackmail. We had to give in to the demands of the former provincial capitals for county status so that they would support the new number of provinces."[54] This political compromise pushed the total number of county-level units to 373.[55]

These particular outputs of territorial reforms on the county level have resulted in several unintended outcomes for this part of the reform. With the establishment of so many cities with county status came the creation of what are called "donut" counties surrounding forty-six of these cities. According to government and other reports, these "donut" counties are effectively cut off from the city infrastructure and resources they had come to rely on, leaving them among the poorest and least successful of all counties in Poland.[56] This was one reason for the increase in disparity between urban and nonurban areas. Another reason was that almost immediately there arose a difference between county services provided in cities with county status and those provided in regular counties. This is attributed to the fact that cities could use municipal funds to supplement county funds while regular counties did not have this option.

In terms of the number of counties one study on the first two years of the reform states, "the number of counties is clearly dysfunctional because the units are too small, weak economically and in terms of staff, and the majority are not in a state to effectively fulfill all the tasks laid on them."[57] The territorial division of the state into many small counties has already had a negative influence on the successful realization of administrative decentralization. Predictions that the large number of small counties will result in weak county democracy are yet to be tested because fiscal decentralization has not yet been implemented (see discussion on fiscal decentralization in this chapter).

Provinces

The final number of provinces was determined in the last stage almost solely by political interests. Government officials, backed by expert scholars from the Institute of Public Affairs, came up against the left coalition and some members of their own right coalition who were pressured by their constituencies not to liquidate specific provinces as proposed by the government. In addition, President Aleksander Kwaśniewski (a social democrat) worked against the government's proposal by apparently using his veto power in this particular instance to secure a broad interpretation of presidential veto powers.

While there was much controversy surrounding the exact number of provinces, there was little dispute over the idea of reducing the number of provinces in general. Historical and international influences were key in establishing a broad consensus on this point.[58] Neotraditionalism thus played a role because Poland had a history of large regions, which provided pressure for their return. Indeed, there were seventeen large provinces as recently as 1975, which the communist party abolished with the administrative reforms of that year.[59]

Most influential, however, appeared to be international factors. The Council of Europe's European Charter on Regional Self-Government, though not stipulating the size of a region, had many regulations interpreted by reformers to mean that fairly large units were being called for. In Poland's case reformers determined this to be between twelve and fourteen provinces.[60] The EU actually recommended to Poland that the territorial division of the state needed to be improved in order to implement structural funds.[61] Reformers also took into consideration EU statistical regions, in this case the fact that provinces should correspond to NUTS-2 statistical regions in EU countries. Poland was also concerned that provinces be large enough to compete economically with regions in Western Europe and be able to represent themselves on equal footing in the EU's Committee on Regions.[62]

In the end, reformers established eight official criteria a region had to possess in order to be established, a few of which are outwardly international or historical in nature:

1 Accessibility to funds (eligibility of the region for outside funds, i.e. EU structural funds);
2 Economic self-sufficiency;
3 Different types of economic sources, namely industries;
4 A market;
5 A cohesive infrastructure;
6 Tradition and culture;
7 The existence of an academic center;
8 A strong metropolis.[63]

Adherence to these guidelines, a little political maneuvering within the coalition itself, and influences as noted above resulted in the twelve provinces the right coalition presented for a vote in parliament.[64]

Political interests, however, did not allow the final number of provinces to be determined along these mostly rational lines. Despite the right coalition's political compromise with former provincial capitals in granting them "city with county status," local protests against the liquidation of a number of provinces gained momentum as voting on the number of provinces proceeded. This placed a lot of pressure on members of parliament not to pass legislation calling for only twelve provinces. The right coalition itself was divided on the matter and did not have a majority of the votes to pass the legislation. In addition to pressure from provinces that were to be liquidated, many of the smaller parties in AWS did not want to give up the privilege the coalition had of appointing the forty-nine *voivods* (governors over central administration offices on the provincial level). They also outwardly protested that consolidation of provinces would undermine the development of grass roots parties.[65] Even the party leadership of the AWS was initially in favor of fifteen to seventeen provinces because it was seen as more politically feasible than twelve. Indeed, one reformer, Jan Maria Rokita, noted that AWS had never treated the reform in terms of consequences for the country but rather in terms of building internal support for AWS. However, government experts were convincing in their claim that sixteen to seventeen provinces would prove harmful to the country, and the coalition presented twelve provinces in parliament. The opposition, namely the social democrats, used the opportunity of division within the right coalition to pressure for more provinces to satisfy the political pressure it was feeling on the issue. However, its party was also divided, and in order to force a majority that would undermine the vote for twelve provinces, it instituted strict party discipline requiring even those in favor of twelve to vote against it. In the end a law establishing fifteen provinces was sent for presidential approval.[66]

Here the story takes another turn. President Alexander Kwaśniewski, of the Democratic Left Alliance (SLD), saw an opportunity for not only gaining political support but also to establish the legal boundaries within which the president can veto a parliamentary law. Even with the passage of fifteen provinces, social protests were still underway in defense of several provinces that would be abolished with the legislation as it stood. In addition, the law at the time this legislation was put before President Kwaśniewski did not state clearly whether the president had the right to veto only where the law touches upon the president's constitutional prerogatives or whether the president can veto any legislation without specific legal justification. Thus, in vetoing the legislation for fifteen provinces his official justification was that he could not approve of a measure that caused such social unrest—that such a law had to take into account economic as well as political and social criteria. His unofficial reason was apparently to establish legal precedence for broader presidential powers—that the president has the right to veto every law. The right coalition did not take the case to the state tribunal to question the constitutionality of this action because they reasoned deliberation would stretch out for years, and in that time another government would come to power. Thus, if they took that route the reform would never take place regardless of the verdict. The right coalition in the end accepted sixteen provinces, and that was the number passed into law.[67]

In terms of unintended consequences, despite fears to the contrary, the establishment of sixteen rather than twelve provinces did not appear to significantly hamper provincial administrative functioning in the first two years of the reform.[68] However, there was significant concern that the larger number would have long-term effects on the general success of not only the new provinces that were added but also on the functioning of the whole provincial system. In particular, the addition of three weak provinces simultaneously weakens four other provinces and increases from two to five the number of provinces without a national border.[69]

Fiscal Decentralization

One of the main goals of reformers was the decentralization of public finances as stipulated in the Polish Constitution. Within the government itself, however, tension arose between those espousing a neotraditional approach supported by a Western ideology of decentralization and top officials in the Ministry of Finance with a neoliberal approach to decentralization. Self-government politicians and government officials saw fiscal decentralization as the key to the return of autonomous functioning of subnational units and the realization of true subsidiarity. This approach was supported by Western European supranational organizations as part of administrative and political decentralization (see discussion under administrative decentralization in this chapter) and the U.S. Agency for International Development (USAID). Even the European Union was clear in its expectation, though not requirement, that fiscal decentralization should take place.[70] Thus, it was long planned that fiscal decentralization would occur in January, 1999, along with implementation of the rest of the public administration reform.

Leszek Balcerowicz, minister of finance, and newly appointed Undersecretary of State for Fiscal Decentralization Jerzy Miller were neoliberals in favor of decentralizing finances to lower levels but reluctant to part with the full amount of funds that decentralization entailed. Indeed, they had every reason to hang on to funds due to the current expense of large reforms, budget deficits, foreign loans coming due, and the need to maintain control over the country's finances in a growing global economy.[71] As staunch neoliberals in their own right, they may have also ascribed to World Bank and International Monetary Fund (IMF) leanings on this matter.[72] Both the World Bank and the IMF fear that "the decentralization of social sector finance responsibilities during structural adjustment efforts are particularly dangerous for macroeconomic stability."[73] The Ministry thus tried to keep as many funds as it could on the central level by funding services at lower levels after they were decentralized.[74] Decentralization done in this manner may be particularly beneficial because it frees up funds for central government use. In addition, Jerzy Miller wanted to "push the envelope" on fiscal decentralization, that is, move it in the direction of privatization, which went beyond what self-government reformers wanted for the reform.[75]

Initially, Kulesza's overburdened office was placed in charge of the fiscal end of the reform. However, a couple of months into reform development the government handed over this responsibility to the Ministry of Finance, because Kulesza's office was unable to cope with the task and because it was thought the fiscal aspect of different reforms could be better coordinated from that ministry. This transfer occurred with the understanding that Kulesza would still be involved in the reform's development.[76]

Within the Ministry of Finance the Department of Local Government Finance had worked on fiscal decentralization projects for many years. Much of this work was supported by funding, expertise, and training provided by the USAID. Two of the main difficulties the department ran into was the high administrative cost of allowing each subnational government to collect its own share of personal income tax (PIT) and the fact that in 1990 municipalities had been given wide-ranging tax authority in many areas.[77] Taking this tax authority from them would mean the loss of municipal support for the overall reform.[78] The department worked with members of parliament and was generally in favor of fiscal decentralization that would keep money in public hands and not privatization.

When Jerzy Miller, in the newly created Office of Undersecretary of State for Fiscal Decentralization (directly subordinate to Leszek Balcerowicz), came into the Ministry of Finance, he came into conflict with this department. Matters came to a head over education finance. Miller advocated school vouchers, which the head of the department opposed on the grounds it would destabilize the public finance system.[79] Miller removed the head of the department and allowed little participation of the department in reform development.[80] Miller also excluded Kulesza on the grounds he was largely ignorant about reform finance.[81] In the end Miller restricted participation in work on the reform to himself and a small group of young assistants, though he did contract out projects to a few consultants.[82] In general, he followed the neoliberal practice of excluding other policymakers to advance policy that he thought would be for the good of all.

In spring, 1998, Miller introduced a fiscal decentralization project that was immediately viewed as inadequate and misleading. In particular, it was misleading about how much money new subnational governments would actually receive with the plan and generally "suggested that the government was looking to use the moment of fiscal decentralization as a way to force a more general reduction of public spending."[83] Needless to say, the project did not gain the support of self-government politicians and the government. The project in any case was impeded by the slow progress of the reform in other areas (such as the decision on the number of provinces and administrative decentralization) and a growing uneasiness among members of parliament over how much fiscal decision-making authority should actually be given to new, untested subnational governments.[84] With time running out the government decided to put off fiscal decentralization and drew up a temporary law on local finances for the first two years of the reform.

With the temporary law, fiscal decision-making remained centralized; funds already earmarked by the ministry for specific decentralized services or service areas were transferred from the central government to new subnational levels for them to distribute. Many justified the two-year delay in fiscal decentralization by arguing it would allow reformers to design a better financial system because they could base it on new government entities and administrations that were actually in place. Delaying fiscal decentralization was also deemed a safer approach because any mistakes in financing could be resolved relatively easily if all funds were still controlled by the center.[85] Another justification was that other countries had waited with fiscal decentralization when undertaking administrative reforms.[86]

With the temporary law self-government politicians and government officials expected that the same amount of money assigned to tasks before decentralization would be assigned after decentralization. Reformers knew that the success of the reform rested in large part on the adequate financing of new subnational governments and their responsibilities. When the first hint of underfunding became apparent, Kulesza stressed that such a situation "could lead to unintended negative social consequences" especially in the case of counties where "financial lack sometimes appears to a degree that threatens the execution of public tasks."[87] Nonetheless Miller was able to fund services at lower levels after they were decentralized, a manipulation that was apparently facilitated by the exclusive control he kept over reform development.[88] Indeed, Miller's view of his expert role continued to result in a lack of consultation with other reformers, including Kulesza, members of parliament, and representatives of subnational governments.[89] When disagreement arose over the final fiscal project for the reform (revealed by Miller only after its completion), Miller stood firm and refused to make any changes. Several times need for compromise was so great and resistance from Miller so strong that it took a meeting with the premier, Jerzy Buzek, to induce him to make any changes.[90] Interestingly, Balcerowicz never reprimanded Miller for his approach. Members of parliament caught inconsistencies in final projects they were given and were able to call the ministry on what they believed were all of them. Nonetheless, everyone was surprised to find the extent to which decentralized services went underfunded after the reform.[91]

For the first quarter of the reform the Association for the Support of Counties calculated the ministry withheld up to 20 percent of funds for decentralized services. Later, unofficial accounts estimate the ministry withheld 25 percent of funding for direct services and 75 percent of funds for investment during the decentralization transition.[92] When the extent of underfunding came to light the ministry justified its actions by stating that local governments are better able to rationalize funding expenditures than the central government and therefore could make do with less. Such rationalization, they argued, was after all in line with reform goals. Some pointed to experience with municipalities that had shown local governments were able to provide similar services for less than the central government.[93] Often overlooked, however, was the fact that subnational governments are able to rationalize expenditures only when they have the freedom to move funds around, a freedom greatly lacking with the temporary fiscal law. Needless to say, new subnational governments immediately complained of a serious lack of money to cover tasks handed down to them from the central government.[94]

There is also evidence the reform actually resulted in increased fiscal centralization rather than fiscal decentralization in Poland. The level of decentralized public finances fell from 12.2 percent of the entire public finance sector in 1998 (which then included only municipalities) to 11.8 percent in 2000 (which included municipalities, counties, and provinces). This reflects the fact that subnational self-governments received almost no new authority over public finances with the reform and the sector as a whole lost authority. When simultaneously taking into consideration the fact that the percentage of expenditures made by self-government units in relation to the entire public finance sector rose from 15.6 percent in 1998 to 22.4 percent in 2000, it is evident that new self-government units are indeed being funded by transfers from the central government.[95]

In spring, 2000, Jerzy Miller, still as undersecretary of state in the Ministry of Finance, made another attempt at a permanent law on fiscal decentralization but again kept its development behind closed doors. When a draft of the law was revealed, self-government reformers, including many members of parliament, could not agree with how the law would take tax revenue authority from the municipalities and give it to counties as well as with "equalization" measures that would redistribute funds from the richest to the poorest subnational units. In particular the draft project called for dispensing with education and road block grants and replacing them with participation in state tax revenues. Such a change would mean the loss of a central government guarantee that funds for these services would always be provided. Due to the overwhelming disapproval of the draft legislation it did not gain the approval of the government and was never considered in parliament.[96] It was during this time that the Freedom Union left the coalition with the Solidarity Electoral Action and removed all their ministers from the government—including Balcerowicz as minister of finance. Miller did not belong to the Freedom Union (nor to any party), but after the defeat of his second proposal for fiscal decentralization he voluntarily left his post.

The underfunding of decentralized services and the lack of fiscal decentralization had significant consequences for administrative and political decentralization respectively. For administrative decentralization the underfunding of services meant, in a large number of cases, the incomplete implementation of newly decentralized services and thus unmet needs of citizens.[97] For political decentralization the lack of fiscal decentralization meant limited autonomous functioning and thus limited potential for democracy in newly elected county and provincial governments. With fiscal decision-making still undertaken by the center, new subnational governments had little authority to make changes in services according to the wishes of their constituencies. Those in new county and provincial governments discovered soon after the reform that without their own funds they had very little power.[98]

The 1999 public administration reform in Poland was affected by a host of factors, from historical, institutional, international, and political influences to the need for political compromises that often produced negative reform outcomes. This was particularly the case with the compromise over the number of counties, where the large number of counties and cities with county status increased disparities between urban and nonurban areas and undermined the efficient functioning of counties. Moreover, poor outcomes in one area of the reform often negatively influenced outcomes in other areas of the reform. The most striking example of this was found with fiscal decentralization. Here top officials in the Ministry of Finance came into tension with other government officials and politicians pushing for adequate decentralization of funds. The resulting underfunding of newly decentralized services had serious consequences for implementation of these services and thus administrative decentralization. The delay of fiscal decentralization, in general, negatively influenced political decentralization as it resulted in limited autonomy and precluded potential democracy in newly established county and provincial self-governments. Overall, a comparison of county and provincial reforms showed that county reforms were shaped more by domestic forces while provincial reforms were more influenced by international pressures, both directly and indirectly.

5 Analysis of Policy and Outcomes for Social Service Delivery

The preceding discussion on the politics of the public administration reform and its broad impact on outcomes uncovered ways in which large-scale pressures and processes impacted on the reform as a whole. As alluded to, however, each individual public service area was affected not only by these more macro-scale events but also by processes specific to each service area. This analysis takes as its next step an evaluation of policy and outcomes in the area of social service delivery to illustrate how both overarching reform policy and service-specific policy affected outcomes for citizens.

The area of social services encompasses a broad array of service types and funding arrangements, which makes it more representative of public services on the whole than other areas. Social services under consideration here mainly include those benefits and programs that were decentralized to or newly established on county and provincial levels.[1] On the county level this includes all types of social assistance homes and the new county family assistance center responsible for crisis intervention, specialized counseling, services for the disabled, foster care, and community integration services for youth, among others. Provinces, rather than administer programs, were entrusted with regional development and education programs for social services with the addition of a provincial social service administrative office under the auspices of new provincial self-government. Old centrally run provincial offices retained their monitoring and supervisory role. This chapter analyzes goals, politics, policies, and outcomes with respect to overarching structural reforms that impacted on social service delivery and legislation specific to social service delivery created with the reform. Data on policy outcomes is provided by a nationwide, representative survey of public social service institutions on three levels of government and other post-reform studies of social services in Poland.

The public administration reform in Poland was undertaken largely on the basis of expected improvements to democracy and public services and therefore had important implications for the social service delivery system. Zaucha, a Polish author, stated, "The main purpose in introducing counties is to make the rest of the social service system ... which is now under central control, more efficient and economically sound by putting it under the scrutiny of its own customers and clients."[2] The goals of the reform are therefore easily applied to the social service context.

As presented earlier, the original goals of the reform included:

1. the continuation of public management decentralization
2. expansion of civil society mechanisms, democracy, and societal control (monitoring) over administrative activities
3. the greater effectiveness of institutions providing public services on a nationwide as well as local scale
4. improvement in the rationality of public expenditures
5. reconstruction of the public finance system and improvement of its cohesiveness
6. to bring order to the public administration competency system and a correction in the flow of information
7. creation of instruments to conduct regional politics
8. bring efficiency to central government functioning, modernize central government administration in the center and in the field
9. development of a professional civil service
10. make possible the natural advance of the political elite (from municipal government through county and provincial government to the national level)
11. adaptation of the country's territorial organization to European Union standards[3]

Goals 1 through 7 and 9 can be translated directly into goals in the area of social service delivery. The following are these goals rewritten in the context of social service delivery and categorized by their relation to democracy and improved public services:

DEMOCRACY

A Increased decentralization of social service tasks (goal 1)

B Appropriate and rational funding for social service tasks (goals 4, 5)

C Increased influence of civil society and societal control over social services (goal 2)
D Increased influence of democracy (county elections) on county social service tasks (goal 2)

IMPROVED PUBLIC SERVICES

A Improvement in social services in terms of distance and accessibility (goal 3)
B Improvement in the clarity of the competency system and flow of information (goal 6)
C Addition of regional politics and planning in the area of social services (goal 7)
D Improvement in the level of professionalism in local social services (goal 9)

The Social Service Delivery System before and after Reform

Efforts to realize the goals of the reform with respect to social services dramatically changed Poland's system of social service delivery. Prior to the reform, social services were organized in a three-tiered hierarchical system (see figure 1). The Ministry of Labor and Social Policy directly oversaw the functioning of forty-nine provincial social assistance offices, which in turn monitored and provided assistance to 2,489 municipal social assistance centers. Provincial offices were essentially central government field offices while municipal centers divided their work between tasks delegated and funded by the central government and tasks given to them as a legal mandate and funded by the municipality (though the distinction between delegated and "own" tasks and fiscal responsibility for them was at times unclear).[4] Provincial offices also had direct oversight over social assistance homes for the elderly, the developmentally disabled, and mentally ill, as well as orphanages, services for the disabled, and most day homes and rehabilitation centers.[5] Adoption and family foster care arrangements were handled through the education system on the provincial level. Duties of municipal social assistance centers involved the disbursement of social welfare benefits and other programs to meet the immediate material needs of poor citizens.

The 1999 reform changed the public service system from this

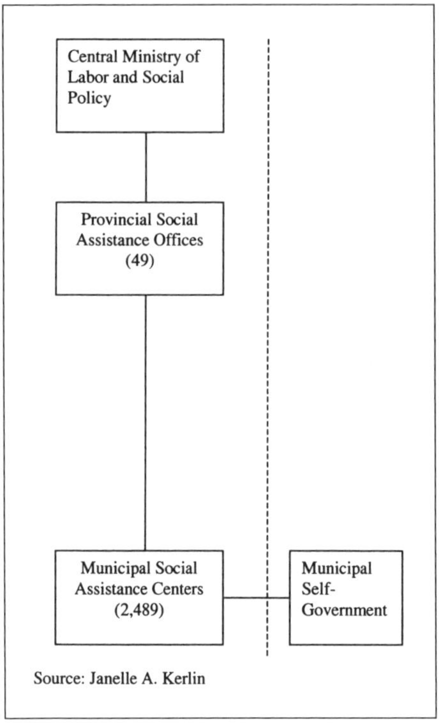

Figure 1. Old social service delivery structure, 1990–98

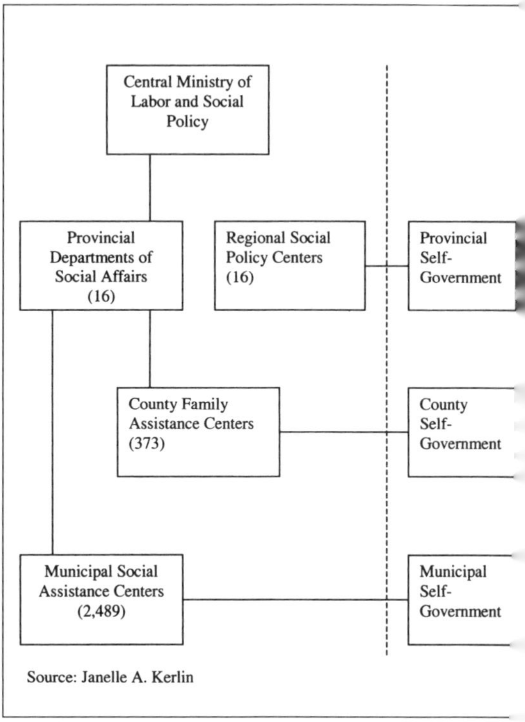

Figure 2. Social service delivery structure after the 1999 public administration reform

three-tiered hierarchical system to a four-tiered system of mostly horizontal and complementary administrative units (see figure 2). It restored the county level to include 308 regular counties and 65 cities with county status. Counties were established as local self-governing administrative units that are complementary rather than hierarchical in relation to municipalities. That is, rather than oversee the activities of municipalities they are only responsible for local services that are best provided on a scale larger than the municipality. In fact, this reform made no legal changes to the municipality; decentralization at this time occurred only at county and provincial levels.[6] On the provincial level the reform introduced sixteen provinces to replace the forty-nine in existence. Both self-government and central government institutions were established in the provinces, making them simultaneously hierarchical and complementary in nature.[7]

For social services, the 1999 reform brought sweeping changes not only to the administration of services but also to the kinds of services social service reformers envisioned for new provincial and county social service institutions. Responsibility for most of the tasks covered previously by the forty-nine provincial social assistance offices was decentralized to the newly restored county level. In the 308 regular counties such services were placed under the jurisdiction of new county family assistance centers while in the sixty-five cities with county status they were given to city social assistance centers who with the reform took on both municipal and county responsibilities. Decentralized services included social assistance homes for the elderly, the developmentally disabled, and mentally ill, orphanages, services for the disabled, specialized counseling, and some day homes and rehabilitation centers. Reformers also took responsibility for adoptions and foster care from the education system and placed it in social services on the county level. In addition, they mandated for the first time certain underdeveloped services including crisis intervention centers and the provision of information on rights to services and placed them on the county level.

As on the municipal level, tasks were divided between those the central government delegated to the county to administer but continued to fund and oversee (commissioned tasks) and those the county took over as its own legal responsibility (county tasks) with some tasks still funded by the central government and others funded by the county. The division between these tasks is loosely based on those services that are monetary benefits for eligible recipients (these are commissioned tasks, such as direct financial aid for foster children) and those tasks that require programming (county tasks, such as specialist counseling or help with integration). A trend in the year 2000, one year after the reform, saw additional tasks changed from a commissioned to a county status.[8]

Two public social service institutions were established in each of the sixteen provinces as a result of the dual system of government on this level. One institution, the Department of Social Affairs, is an entity functioning within provincial central government offices. The other, most often called the regional social policy center, operates under the auspices of provincial self-government. The Department of Social Affairs is mainly concerned with the disbursement of funds and monitoring of those tasks the central government has commissioned to county and municipal levels. Regional social policy centers, which were optional for provincial self-governments, plan social programs on the regional level and plan and support the education of social service workers.

Evaluation of the New Social Service Delivery System

Prior to the research presented in this study, studies to determine outcomes of these broad reforms to social services were narrow in scope or unrepresentative of the situation in the country as a whole. In the summer of 1999 the Ministry of Labor and Social Policy contracted out a study on county family assistance centers that, while representative of new county family assistance centers in the 308 regular counties, did not address the situation in the sixty-five cities with county status, where a large proportion of the population resides. It also did not assess the functioning of the two social service offices on the provincial level. In addition, the study was conducted only half a year after the reform package was implemented and failed to test certain hypotheses of the reform.[9] Another study completed by the Institute of Applied Social Sciences at the University of Warsaw for the Ministry of Internal Affairs and Administration based conclusions about county-level reform on case studies of only four county family assistance centers.[10] Likewise, an inspection report prepared in May, 2000, by Poland's state auditing office was brief and included only seventeen county family assistance centers.[11] For the most part, where research topics overlap, these studies substantiate research finding presented here and vice versa.

To fill in the gaps in the research on outcomes for social services after decentralization the author conducted a nationwide representative survey during summer, 2000, of directors of two hundred public social service institutions on three levels of government. Research was conducted one and a half years after reform implementation first began in January, 1999; expectations for outcomes were thus moderated against the early timing of the study. Indeed, the study in no way attempted a final evaluation of the reform in the area of social services but was intended as a snapshot of a moment in a dynamic process expected to extend over many years.

Institutions in the study included sixty-six municipal social assistance centers, seventy county family assistance centers, thirty-two city family assistance centers, all sixteen provincial departments of social affairs, and all sixteen provincial regional social policy centers. These institutions were selected as follows. A random representative sample of sixty-six county family assistance centers (out of 308) was conducted and yielded fifty-seven survey responses.[12] To offset refusals a random re-sampling of thirteen additional county centers was done and resulted in a final count of seventy completed county surveys with an overall response rate of 88.6 percent. A random sample of thirty-three city family assistance centers (out of sixty-five) resulted in thirty-two completed surveys for a response rate of 97 percent. No re-sampling was done in this category. Municipalities were selected from the initial sixty-six counties sampled above, with one municipality randomly sampled from each county (there are on average three to five municipalities in a county). In the case of a refusal another municipality was randomly sampled from the same county. For the two institutions on the provincial level, sixteen out of sixteen provincial departments of social affairs and sixteen out of sixteen regional social policy centers completed surveys for a response rate of 100 percent in each case. On county and provincial levels self-administered questionnaires consisting of close ended questions were delivered by an interviewer who remained present during survey completion.[13] Surveys conducted in municipalities were done by computer-assisted telephone interviewing (CATI) using fixed-response questions.[14] Survey instruments were developed by the author in Polish with the consultation of many Polish experts including practitioners, researchers, and government officials in social services (see appendix C for the county survey in English and Polish). A Polish research institute, Pracownia Badań Społecznych, provided trained interviewers and initial data analysis.[15]

The two purposes of the survey were to determine the degree to which overall goals of the public administration reform had been achieved in the area of social services and to identify any unexpected, especially adverse, outcomes in relation to those goals. Survey questions were accordingly built to identify outcomes in these two broad areas. The goals of the reform provided an overall framework for the formulation of survey questions. A small open-ended survey of county and municipal social service institutions helped to further inform survey topics, especially in the area of unexpected outcomes of the reform. The result was a list of question topics for the surveys:

1. Degree of decentralization/reform implementation for social service tasks in cities with county status and counties (goal 1)
2. Funding for social service tasks in cities with county status and counties (goals 4, 5)
3. Influence of civil society and societal control over social services (goal 2)
4. Influence of democracy (county elections) on county social service tasks (goal 2)
5. Improvement in social services in terms of distance and accessibility (goal 3)
6. Improvement in the flow of information (goal 6)
7. Regional politics and planning in the area of social services (goal 7)
8. Improvement in the level of professionalism in local social services (goal 9)

The author hypothesized that decentralization would be incomplete due to under-implementation of social services; that services would be underfunded; that the reform would have little influence on civil society in the sphere of social services due to lack of initiative and resources to collaborate (on the part of both civil society actors and public officials); that societal control over services would be minimal; that elected county government would also have minimal influence over services; that the flow of information between levels of government would worsen due to the addition of administrative offices and the formal autonomy of subnational self-governments; that it would be too early for regional offices to have fully operating regional plans for social services; and that professionalization in county social services would be low due to lack of educated and experienced workers and an increase in politicization.

Potential bias in the study stems from the fact that directors of social service institutions were the main source of information. Here directors may have produced results skewed towards more positive outcomes because they may have been inclined to show positive portraits of themselves and the programs they oversee. As will be shown, however, an overview of survey results indicates that directors consistently provided both positive and even very negative responses, which indicates that director bias was probably minimal. During survey development, however, one question on the politicization of county social service directors was particularly suspect to generate biased results. Such bias is taken into consideration in the analysis of that survey response.

Limitations of the survey also generally include the need for more in-depth consideration of some of the covered subjects. In particular, the survey was unable to gather specific information on services with mixed funding (funded by both central and subnational governments) and precise funding levels of services in general. The survey was also limited in its ability to evaluate the quality of implemented tasks, including the quality of programs directed at specific populations, the depth of cooperation of social service institutions with other entities once initiated, and the quality of the needs assessment and goal planning instrument, if completed. A more detailed survey instrument as well as surveys of social service workers and recipients of services would address these limitations but were beyond project feasibility.

Though not a limitation, there was a noticeable age difference among directors depending on which social service institution they were from. In urban areas (cities with county status and counties immediately surrounding them) about 85 percent of directors of county and city family assistance centers were over forty years of age. In more rural counties and in municipalities (without county status) directors were younger, with 60 percent of directors over forty years old.

Analysis of Reform Policy and Outcomes

Analysis of the policies that created the social service delivery system described above shows they were not always written in a manner supportive of achieving stated goals of the reform. Policies fell into three categories: deviant policy (policy that did not achieve its intended goal); counterproductive policy (policy that addressed the intended goal but worked at cross purposes with other goals); and expected policy. These types of policies were found on the level of overarching structural changes to the administrative system that impacted social service delivery and on the level of specific social policy legislation. The analysis makes a distinction between the outputs of the reform and its outcomes. Outputs are the number of services or amount of benefits provided or other activities completed by social service personnel in the course of implementing public policy. Outcomes are the fulfillment of reform goals or unintended consequences of the reform, in this case, in the area of social services.[16] Low outputs and disparities in outputs between different geographical areas and types of social service organizations in the study provided insight on policy outcomes and thus goals of the reform. The analysis is not intended to be an exhaustive survey of all social service policy and outcomes associated with the reform but rather an overview of some of the main failures and successes of the reform in this area. The discussion draws upon the information obtained in the author's survey as well as the research conducted by Polish institutions mentioned above.

Deviant Policy

Fiscal Policy. Large-scale reform processes in the area of fiscal policy worked to undermine reform goals with respect to social services. Fiscal policy was intended to cover the needs of decentralized services and provide for the autonomous (potentially democratic) functioning of subnational units—that is, that citizens, through their local governments, would be more involved in decisions regarding decentralized services. Due to the politics of the reform, administrative tasks were decentralized but fiscal responsibility was not, which effectively retained decision-making power regarding services on the central level.[17] Moreover, some services went largely underfunded. Thus, the temporary fiscal policy put in place with the reform was not in harmony with its goals of adequate funding of subnational services and improved democracy.

With the temporary fiscal policy, funding from the central government for decentralized services (including commissioned and some county tasks) came in the form of a targeted grant *(dotacja)* or a more flexible subsidy *(subwencja)* for a whole service area. In this way the central government largely retained both revenue-generating and revenue-assignment authority over finances. Most of the funding for social services came in the form of targeted grants. However, the county was given complete fiscal responsibility for some social services and was therefore expected to find funding for them even though on average less than 5 percent of a county's budget consisted of its own county funds.[18] This meant that in those cases where fiscal responsibility for decentralized services was given to subnational governments, they were not provided with sufficient revenue-generating capacity nor adequate shares in centrally controlled personal income tax (PIT) and corporate income tax (CIT) to finance tasks for which they had been given fiscal responsibility.[19] There was thus a great disproportion between the cost of decentralized county tasks and the level of fiscal decentralization needed for counties to be able to support these tasks out of their own revenue. This situation was the case with respect to over half the tasks (those regarded as "county" as opposed to "commissioned") assigned to newly established county family assistance centers. The result was dramatic underfunding of these services and thus limited implementation and minimal power in the hands of elected county and provincial officials to direct services according to local preferences.

The author's survey assessed the level of funding and degree of implementation for devolved (county) and centrally funded (commissioned) services. For county social service tasks (funded by the county at the time of the survey), seven out of nine such tasks were evaluated. They included provision of specialist counseling, development of a county strategy for solving social problems, operation of a crisis intervention center, training and professional development of social service staff, case consultation with municipal social service centers, financing of county support centers (except those for the mentally ill), and help with integration for youth leaving institutions. The survey found that in regular counties county funds covered 21 percent of need with regard to these seven county tasks.[20] The picture is somewhat improved when looking at cities with county status. Here city funds covered 47 percent of need with respect to the seven tasks (see figure 3).[21] The disparity between regular counties and cities with county status in the area of county tasks is the result of a counterproductive policy discussed below.

Commissioned tasks that were still funded by the central government were funded at much higher levels. However, there were also fewer commissioned tasks, and most involved benefit transfers to specific populations rather than funds for programming. Three

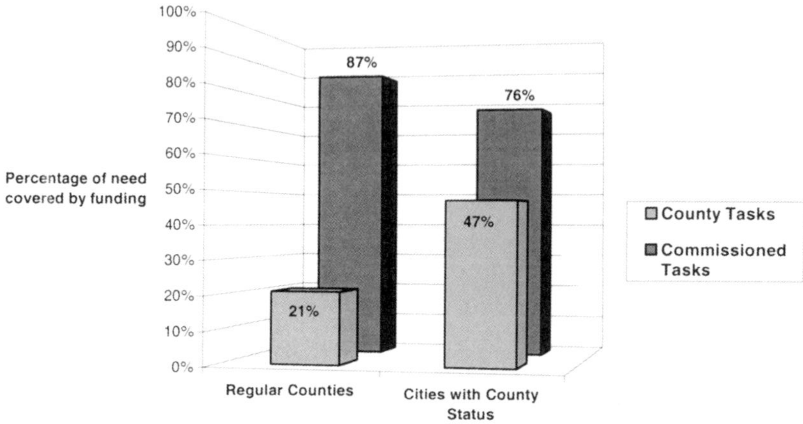

Figure 3. Percentage of need covered by funding with regard to county and commissioned social service tasks, 1999

commissioned tasks lent themselves to the present analysis.[22] They were the provision of financial aid for the maintenance of children in foster families, provision of financial aid for youth leaving institutions, and payment of salaries for county workers realizing central government tasks. In regular counties central government funds covered 87 percent of need with regard to these three commissioned tasks administered by the county.[23] By contrast, in cities with county status central government funds covered 76 percent of need with respect to the three tasks (see figure 3).[24] No substantiated explanation has been found for why there is this disparity between counties and cities with county status in funds for commissioned services.[25] The large difference between funds for county tasks and commissioned tasks is mostly explained by the fact that commissioned tasks are still funded by the central government, whereas county tasks are funded out of county revenue that is not supported by a sufficient level of fiscal decentralization (such as local revenue-generating capacity or adequate shares in PIT and CIT) as discussed. Other reports also cite the lack of funding for county social services found here.[26] These data confirm the author's hypothesis that decentralized social services would be underfunded.

The low degree of implementation for county tasks is in part a reflection of this low level of funding.[27] Survey results showed that only 27 percent of regular counties had fully implemented county tasks with respect to the seven outlined above.[28] This number var-

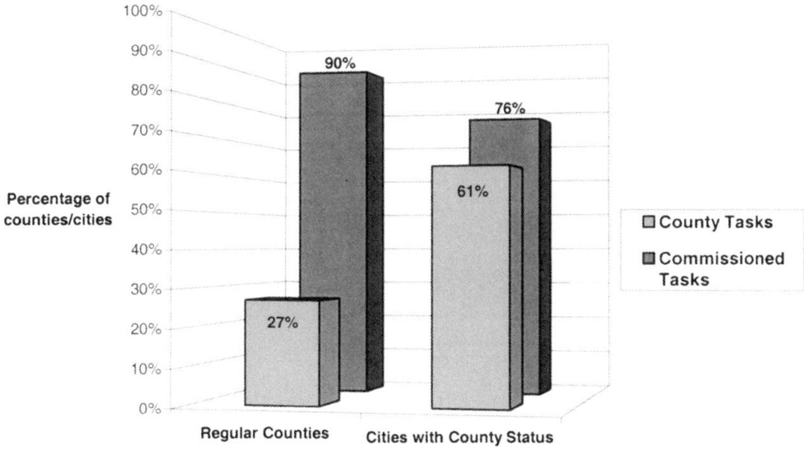

Figure 4. Percentage of counties and cities with county status that have fully implemented county and commissioned social service tasks, July, 2000

ied significantly from cities with county status, where 61 percent of cities had fully implemented county tasks with respect to these seven (see figure 4).[29] Accordingly, the level of implementation for commissioned tasks was much higher. Ninety percent of counties and 76 percent of cities with county status had fully implemented commissioned services on the basis of the three commissioned services listed above (see figure 4).[30] Overall it is apparent that centrally funded commissioned tasks were funded and implemented to a much greater degree than were county tasks left to county funding. These findings are supported by the Polish Ministry of Labor and Social Policy's commissioned report that found that 89 percent of county family assistance centers in regular counties cited the lack of financial resources as a main problem hindering the realization of tasks.[31] Decentralization was incomplete in the area of social services due, at least in part, to the underimplementation of services, a finding that confirms the author's hypothesis in this area.

County and city centers did have some recourse to this dismal fiscal situation. Survey results showed that about two-thirds sought out and used central government and county reserves and about half received help from sponsors. About 40 percent also cooperated with other counties to reduce program costs. Some 36 percent of counties compared to 72 percent of cities cooperated with nongovernmental organizations (NGO) to reduce costs (see figure 5). This

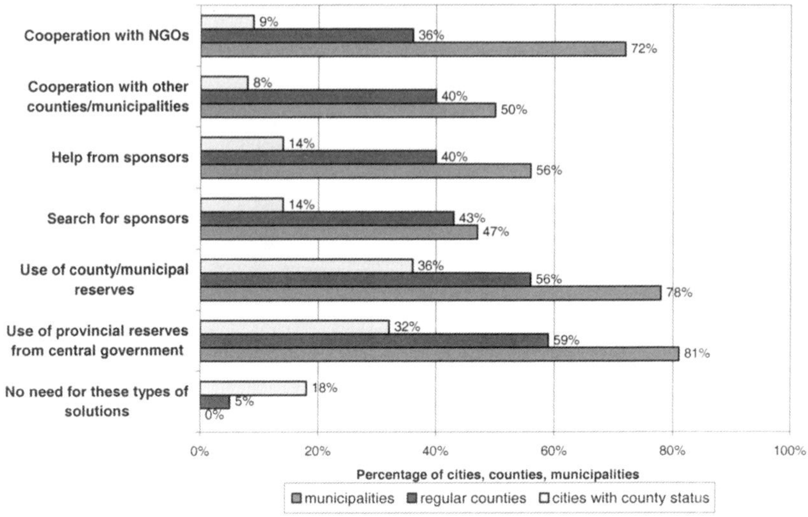

Figure 5. Solutions used when faced with a lack of funds, July, 2000

difference is attributed to the fact that many more nongovernmental organizations are found in cities than in counties (see discussion on civil society below). In addition, 39 percent of surveyed county center directors and 19 percent of city directors indicated they had used central government money assigned to commissioned tasks to fund county tasks that were supposed to be funded by own county revenue, an act that is illegal according to Polish law.

Regional social policy centers, under the auspices of provincial self-government, found themselves in a similar situation with respect to funding for all of their tasks. These tasks included determining the balance of needs and resources in the area of social assistance, implementing and subsidizing targeted programs, operating schools of social service and professional training, identifying the causes of poverty and equalizing the standard of living, and inspiring and promoting new solutions in the area of social policy. The survey showed that two-thirds of all regional social policy center directors indicated that the lack of resources contributed to why these tasks went unrealized or were only partially realized. Here again the lack of fiscal decentralization resulted in the underfunding of services for which the provincial self-government had been given complete responsibility. (Kuzmiuk finds this across many service areas on the provincial level.[32])

Table 3. County Political Party in Power and Level at which Funds Covered Need for County Social Service Tasks, 1999

	Level at which funds covered need for county social service tasks:				
Type of county political party	to 15%	to 24%	to 45%	to 100%	Total
Left/Center-Left	13	10	10	6	39
	33.3%	25.6%	25.6%	15.4%	100%
Right/Center-Right	11	9	7	4	31
	35.5%	29.0%	22.6%	12.9%	100%
Total	24	19	17	10	70
	34.3%	27.1%	24.3%	14.3%	100%

Pearson Chi-Square (3 d.f.) = .238, prob. = .971.
Database: Author's county survey conducted by Pracownia Badań Społecznych, summer, 2000.
Data analysis: Pracownia Badań Społecznych.

Lack of fiscal decentralization also hindered the potential for democracy on subnational levels in that it limited the autonomy of county and provincial self-governments to direct services according to local preferences. In order to assess this aspect of subnational government performance in the area of social services, the county survey included several questions regarding parties and spending on social services. Type of political party in power in the county was then correlated with the amount the county spent on strictly county social service tasks. Analysis found there was no statistically significant association between type of party in power and the extent to which county funds met needs in the area of social services in 1999 (see table 3). This suggests that due to a lack of fiscal decentralization, counties did not receive enough of their own revenue to make a discussion on where money should be spent an important factor reflecting party philosophy. Stated another way, lack of fiscal decentralization and the resulting small revenues of counties made citizen feedback through elected officials a weak instrument of societal control over services. This, under the assumption that county parties on the right and left would respond as traditionally expected, where right parties spend less on social services and left spend more given the same amount of resources. This finding confirms the author's hypothesis that elected county government would have minimal influence over social services.

Commentators on the reform agree with this unfavorable assessment of county government influence on social services in its jurisdiction. Grosse notes that "financial, organizational, and property conditions have limited the functioning of the county to a serious degree.... it does not possess a sufficient budget and above all its 'own' resources allowing for the generation of its own policy in this area [of social services]."[33] Indeed, representatives of the Polish local elite often comment on the lack of "own" funds and therefore autonomy in counties in general. As one official noted, "Self-government without money is a parody of self-government."[34]

Counterproductive Policy

Counterproductive policy is policy that, while achieving its immediate goal, worked at cross purposes with other goals of the reform. This section addresses many of the ironies of the reform in the area of social services by looking at these counterproductive policies. Included here are both overarching reform policy that influenced social services as well as policy specific to the area of social welfare. Here, policy that was most often in line with the goal of decentralization for the purpose of bringing government closer to the people came in conflict with goals of an efficient public administration system. As will be shown, this conflict was often the result of the specific structure and circumstances of a given service area.

Policy on Cities with County Status. The creation of sixty-five cities with county status was an overarching policy that resulted in disparities in the funding of county social services between urban and more rural areas. The introduction of disparities was at odds with goals to improve the overall effectiveness of public institutions and the rationality of the public finance system. As discussed in chapter 3, for political reasons former provincial capitals and large cities were given the status of "city with county status." This meant that the largest urban centers in the country (excluding Warsaw) were allowed to create a county within their city borders. Each of these cities essentially functions as both a municipality and a county with the ability to transfer funds freely between the two budgets. Cities with county status were therefore able to supplement limited county funds for social services with municipal funds. Regular counties, on the other hand, had no parallel legal recourse to draw funds from the budgets of municipalities within their borders (in rural areas these municipalities were often very poor anyway). The result was a built-in disparity for county services between cities with county status and regular counties (see figure 3).

Policy on Provincial Offices. The overarching structure of the reform on the provincial level also appears to have contributed to some inefficiencies in the relationship between the two provincial offices and local social service offices. Before the reform, municipal offices carrying out centrally commissioned tasks were directly subordinate to centrally run provincial social offices of which there were forty-nine. With the reform, the number of provinces (and thus the number of these provincial offices) was reduced to sixteen to achieve the goal of harmonization with Western European countries. A problem arose after the reform because these provincial offices maintained many of the same responsibilities with respect to municipal offices. The result was that in the area of social services the newly renamed provincial departments of social affairs (still under the jurisdiction of the central government) were in effect centralized from the point of view of municipal social assistance centers. The over three hundred county family assistance centers introduced with the reform did not take over the supervisory and support tasks of provincial offices but instead complemented services provided by municipal centers. Fewer provincial departments not only had to supervise and coordinate planning and funding for social service tasks the central government commissioned to municipal centers but also those commissioned to new county family assistance centers. While municipal centers continued to send information on commissioned tasks in the form of formal paper reports, any other communication required a series of phone calls and letters or faxes before an issue was addressed. Indeed, the author's survey also revealed that many municipal center directors felt that contact with provincial departments worsened with the reform and that municipal centers were essentially left on their own. When directors were asked how contact with the provincial department had changed after the reform 49 percent said it was worse or much worse and 41 percent said it remained the same.[35]

Another problem stemming from the overarching structure of the reform involving intergovernmental relationships was found between regional social policy centers (under the jurisdiction of provincial self-government) and county and municipal assistance centers. Similar to the relationship between counties and municipalities, the self-governing side of provincial government was created to be complementary rather than hierarchical in relation to counties and municipalities. This meant that regional social policy centers have no authority to require lower levels of government to comply with their requests. While this helps guarantee the autonomous functioning of lower-level units, a goal of the reform, it threatens to limit the extent to which regional plans and greater efficiency (another goal) can be realized. Thus, policies that state that these centers are, for example, to "develop and implement targeted programs serving the realization of social assistance tasks and their subsidization," are not in agreement with the established structure of the new public administration system and are constrained by it.[36] Indeed, Grosse finds that intergovernmental coordination for these institutions is poor: "A clear shortcoming of present legislation is the insufficient coordination of social policy programming between different levels of local self-government, particularly between the county and provincial self-government."[37]

These findings partially confirm the author's hypothesis that the flow of information between levels of government would grow worse with the reform. While the exchange of information between provincial offices and municipal and county agencies was negatively affected by the reform, it will be shown that there was significant information-sharing between the county and municipal social service offices. The author also hypothesized that it would be too early for regional offices to have fully operating regional plans for social services. This discussion indicates, however, that other factors, such as lack of information and authority to implement regional plans on lower levels, may impede the implementation of regional plans regardless of the amount of time that passes.

Policy on Disability Eligibility Offices and Other Specialized Services. Offices that determine the eligibility of the disabled for social benefits were decentralized to the county level, which brought services much closer to a group of citizens that would have had trouble traveling to now-quite-distant provincial offices. However, the economy of scale appears to have been disrupted for this type of service because the number of citizens needing this service in each county was small and did not justify the establishment of an eligibility office in each county. Reformers foresaw this and suggested in legislation that two or more neighboring counties cooperate and co-finance one office together. As it was only a suggestion,

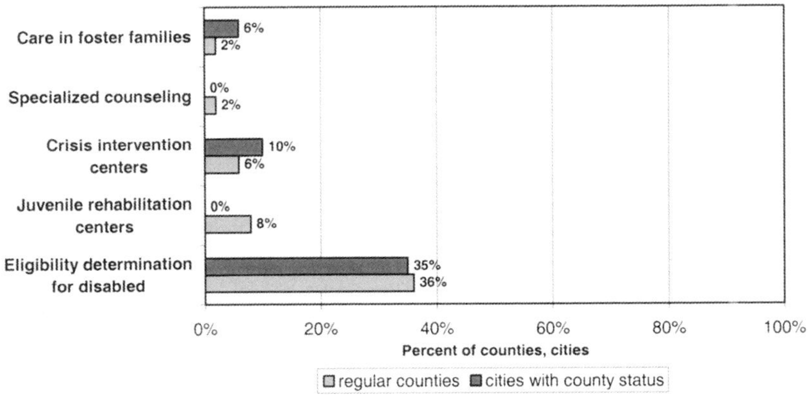

Figure 6. Social services that counties and cities with county status co-finance with other counties, July, 2000

in practice it appears this option was only used when individual counties did not have the funding to operate an office on their own, which made it likely that counties with sufficient funds were operating individual offices at a significant loss in efficiency.[38] This same scenario also appears to be the case for other types of services such as crisis intervention centers, specialized counseling, and juvenile rehabilitation centers. In these cases, though, instead of co-financing when there is a lack of funds, individual county centers offered these services at a poor level or not at all (see figure 6). The fact that co-financing between counties was specifically mentioned in the legislation for benefit eligibility services appears to have influenced eligibility offices to be co-financed at a much higher rate than other social services on the county level. In each case, though, it appears the decentralization of these services disrupted an efficient economy of scale that was not mitigated by self-initiated cooperation between counties.

Policy on Directors of County and City Family Assistance Centers. Policy in the area of social services that calls for the hiring of directors of county and city centers by the head of the county addressed a reform goal aimed at placing authority over programs in the hands of local officials. However, this policy stood at odds with another reform goal to develop a professional civil service to promote efficiency. A professional civil service is one that is highly qualified and is hired based on merit rather than politics. Reform policies for new directors of county and city family assistance centers did not promote such conditions and in fact provided an open door to the increased politicization of social services. Legislation allowed that the elected county head has sole jurisdiction over the hiring and firing of the local director of the county (or city) family assistance center. In addition, the county head was given the authority to intervene in the director's sphere of duties. Indeed, as policy now stands, most social service tasks are legally under the jurisdiction of the county head who then authorizes the center director to make decisions on his behalf.[39] In order to assess the impact of the hiring policy on professionalization, the author's survey looked at whether or not new social service directors in regular counties brought appropriate experience and education to their new positions and whether their hiring was merit- or politically based.

A comparison with municipal center directors helped determine whether new county directors brought more education and experience to social services on the local level after the reform. Results from municipal social assistance centers indicated that directors from these centers had little higher education and only some prior experience in the area of social services, in contrast to county directors, who rated higher in these areas. Specifically, only 36 percent of surveyed municipal directors had achieved the master's level in their education and 42 percent had prior experience in the social service field. On the other hand, of new directors in regular counties, 91 percent had completed a master's degree and 47 percent could claim prior experience in social services (see figure 7).[40] Survey data also indicated that previous work places of county directors were more closely related to other public services or public administration, if not in social services, than those of municipal directors.

With the understanding that a high level of education and experience does not necessarily preclude politicization, the survey attempted to find out whether county directors had been employed based on merit, for political reasons, or both. A comparison was made between responses of directors of city family assistance centers (likely to have been hired before the reform) and directors of county family assistance centers hired with the reform. Interestingly, 87.5 percent of city directors said they were hired based on merit only, and the other 12.5 percent said it was difficult to say. In new counties, however, 74 percent of county directors indicated

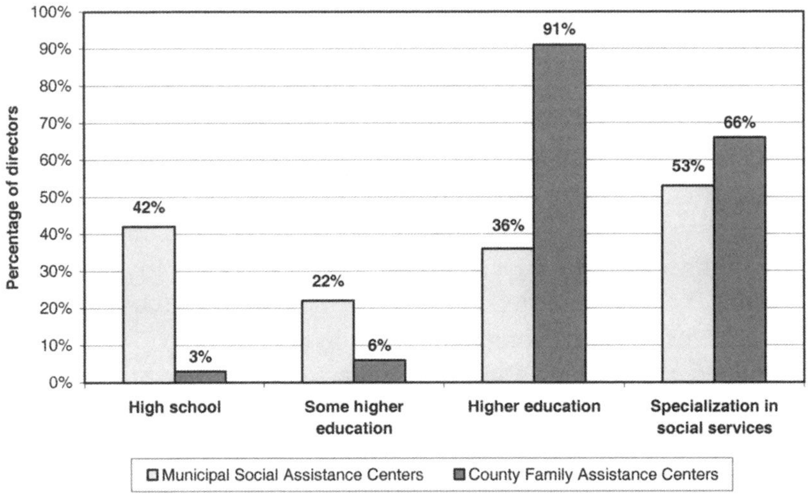

Figure 7. Education of directors of municipal social assistance centers and county family assistance centers (not including directors of city family assistance centers), July, 2000

their employment was merit-based, 15 percent said it was based on both merit and political reasons, and 11 percent indicated it was difficult to say. None of the directors indicated they were hired solely for political reasons, which is supported by the high education and experience of these directors noted above.

While these numbers indicate that only a small amount of politicization may have crept in with the reform, Polish researchers consulted on this matter strongly question whether directors answered this question honestly. Indeed, the president of the Polish National Association of Social Workers strongly felt that after the reform the field became more politicized than these results indicate.[41] Thus, though the policy of allowing county heads to hire directors of county family assistance centers did bring increased professionalization of directors in terms of education and experience, it may have undermined professionalization in other ways by doing little to stop the advance of the politicization of the field. Given this outcome, the author's hypothesis that professionalization in social services would be low in new counties was only partially validated. The one caveat to this discussion is that information on skill level is based only on county directors in comparison to municipal directors. A comparison between other social service workers at the two levels of government may or may not be consistent with these findings.

Policy on Social Assistance Homes. Decentralization of social assistance homes to the county level from the old provincial level came in conflict with other goals to improve the effectiveness of public institutions and the rationality of the public finance system.[42] With the reform, social assistance homes were handed over as the responsibility and property of the county in which they found themselves, though monitoring for adherence to service standards remained the task of provincial departments. Such decentralization, however, immediately appeared to create suboptimal fiscal arrangements and some disparity in service accessibility across counties. Problems arose because the number of institutions and their location remained constant while their service jurisdictions shrunk with the reform. For example, a social assistance home that served a whole province before the reform was given to only one county after the reform, which left the other counties in the former province without an institution of their own. In the worst cases one county would find itself with several institutions while a neighboring county had none. Social assistance homes were willing to admit clients from other counties, but two problems emerged: counties would not, nor could they be expected to, fund residents from other counties in their institutions, and counties with institutions would admit their own residents first, which left applicants from other counties on long waiting lists. Orphanages and juvenile rehabilitation centers faced similar difficulties.

The first problem of how to fund homes that were unequally distributed across counties was solved by writing policy that left fiscal authority for social assistance homes on the central level. This policy approach was supported by politicians who were increasingly wary of handing fiscal responsibility for homes over to local officials who they thought might neglect the needs of home residents.[43] However, such policy came into conflict with reform goals espousing fiscal decentralization and a more rational fiscal system. Algorithms were devised that determined the amount of funding to be spent per person in a social assistance home. A problem then arose about how best to distribute the money—through the home county to whom the money technically belonged or directly to the county where the person was residing in the institution. In a decision made just days before implementation of the reform (set for January 1, 1999) the minister of labor and social policy approved a plan that sent funds to the home county of the individual. The county then transferred the money to its county family assistance center, which then transferred it to the individual's social assistance home wherever it was located. Due to complications with this system, less than half a year later, in June, 1999, this policy was replaced by another that transferred funds directly to the county where the individual resided in the institution.[44]

Other complications using the algorithm method in general appeared, including the leveling of the cost of a place in a social assistance home to the average cost per resident in a given province. This meant that those specialized homes requiring more funding were not able to meet costs while other homes used the situation to overstate their expenses up to the level of the provincial average. The reform's goal of rationalizing finances and providing more effective services was clearly undermined in this instance. In addition, the budget for the operation of social assistance homes was cut from 1,452,079 thousand zloty in 1998 to 1,240,818 thousand zloty in 1999 (the year of the reform), which hampered the success of the reform from the start.[45]

The second problem involving disparities in access to social assistance homes across counties was identified as a difficulty early on, but there was no investigation into how widespread the problem was.[46] Results from the author's survey suggest it was not as far-reaching as officials initially feared. In order to evaluate the accessibility of social assistance homes and juvenile rehabilitation centers the survey asked county and city directors whether accessibility had gotten much worse, worse, the same, better, or much better after the reform.[47] For social assistance homes only 8 percent indicated it had gotten worse or much worse, 31 percent said it had remained the same, and 55 percent said it was better or much better.[48] With regard to juvenile rehabilitation centers, 8 percent were worse off, 42 percent remained the same, and 39 percent had improved.[49] These positive responses, however, may not completely reflect the actual situation because it is not known whether all directors understood the word "accessibility" *(dostępność)* in the same way.[50]

Expected Policy

Expected policy here is understood as policy that shows progress in reaching goals and that doesn't conflict with other goals of the reform. Given the early nature of the study, any movement towards achievement was deemed as an indication that expected policy had been implemented. This section shows how goals of the reform to stimulate civil society, establish increased societal control over public services, and bring services closer to citizens show initial signs of being realized through specific social service policy and activities.

Policy on Cooperation of County Centers with Other Local Entities. Overarching reform policy as well as specific policy in the area of social services aimed at improving civil society did spur on some activity in this area. Civil society, viewed by reformers in a broad sense, includes citizen initiative not mandated by the government and citizen participation (non-mandated) in the development and/or realization of local programs. Decentralization reformers believed that by restoring county units to regions that citizens already culturally identified with, pride in their region would encourage initiative and cooperative efforts.[51] In order to test this hypothesis, the survey attempted to find whether or not new linkages between local social service entities had been introduced with the reform. Specifically, the survey assessed elements of civil society within the social service sphere by identifying the level at which new family assistance centers cooperated with other local entities. In particular, it looked at how much and what kinds of cooperation existed between county centers and municipal social assistance centers and between county or city centers and social service NGOs in the county. The survey and study were conducted with the understanding that civil society of this sort develops very slowly over time.

Despite the fact that municipalities and counties were designed to work parallel to one another, reformers believed that by placing counties on a close level with municipalities the two would, on their own initiative, share information and programming without being legally required to do so.[52] Survey results suggested this is the case, though it appeared to be somewhat one-sided, with county centers more on the receiving end. When directors of municipal centers were asked how well they knew the director of the county family assistance center, 33 percent felt they considered the county center director to be an acquaintance or friend, and 53 percent responded they had spoken many times. Municipal centers indicated they cooperate with county centers in several ways, including developing the county strategy for solving social problems (84 percent), assisting the county center with foster families (78 percent), and identifying people in need of help from the county center (84 percent). Also, half of all municipal center directors said the county center requests informational reports from the municipal center. These findings are supported by a study commissioned by the Polish Ministry of Labor and Social Policy (mentioned previously), which found among other indicators that over 95 percent of polled directors from county centers had an attitude of cooperation and partnership with municipal directors.[53]

Reformers also believed that decentralization of government services would promote increased cooperation with NGOs. Two approaches were taken to evaluate such cooperation: cooperation with formal tasks of the center and cooperation in other center activities. With formal social service tasks, social policy legislation allows, but does not require, that central and local government offices can contract out tasks in the area of social welfare and support them financially.[54] In order to assess the level of cooperation in this area directors were asked which center tasks were realized in cooperation with nongovernmental organizations, whether it was contracting out services, subsidizing NGO services, or informal cooperation. On the basis of nine legislated tasks that best lend themselves to such cooperation, it was determined that 3 percent of family assistance centers (county and city centers together) contract out services, 5 percent subsidize NGO services that fulfill center tasks, and 27 percent have some form of informal cooperation (see figure 8).[55] As the discussion on fiscal policy shows, county and city centers struggled with a lack of basic funds, which appears to be a significant barrier to contracting and subsidization of services. The poor knowledge and experience of practitioners and the lack of formal legal procedures and criteria also contribute to low activity in this area.[56]

The second way cooperation with NGOs was evaluated involved identifying other roles NGOs might have in relation to family assistance centers. Survey results indicated that 39 percent of county

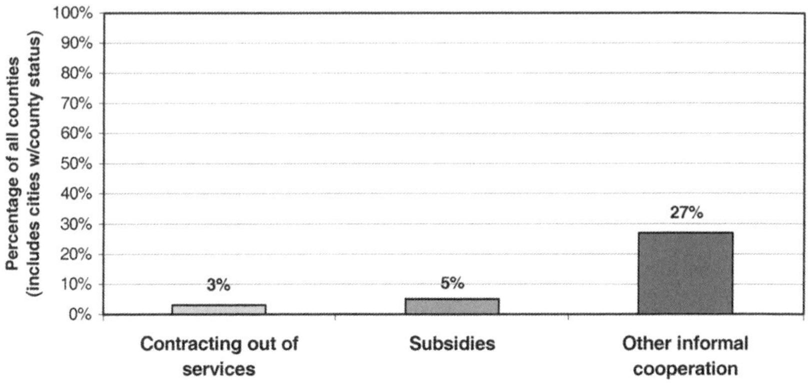

Figure 8. Degree of different forms of cooperation between county and city family assistance centers and social service NGOs with respect to nine legislated tasks, July, 2000

family assistance centers and a surprising 81 percent of city centers cooperate with NGOs in realizing tasks other than those connected with legislated tasks discussed above. The large difference between city and county centers was attributed to the small number of NGOs outside urban areas and that city centers have been in existence a lot longer than county centers. However, examination of other results suggests that regular counties are at times better at utilizing NGOs than city centers. Forty-five percent of county family assistance centers but only 22 percent of city centers said NGOs participate in deciding how money from national funds is divided. Sixty-six percent of county centers and 44 percent of city centers indicated that NGOs provide the center with information on specific social problems. About half of both city and county centers said NGOs serve as advocates for local community social service needs (see figure 9). While city center cooperation with NGOs has had ten or more years to develop, such cooperation in regular counties had, at the time of the survey, only one and a half years to develop. Thus, numbers indicating that about half of all regular counties have NGO involvement in these last three areas is an encouraging sign for civil society development on the new county level. Though reformers were most interested in the contracting out of services to NGOs because of perceived savings (which as indicated stands at only 3 percent of all counties), cooperation in other areas indicates that overall cooperation with social service NGOs has increased with the reform.

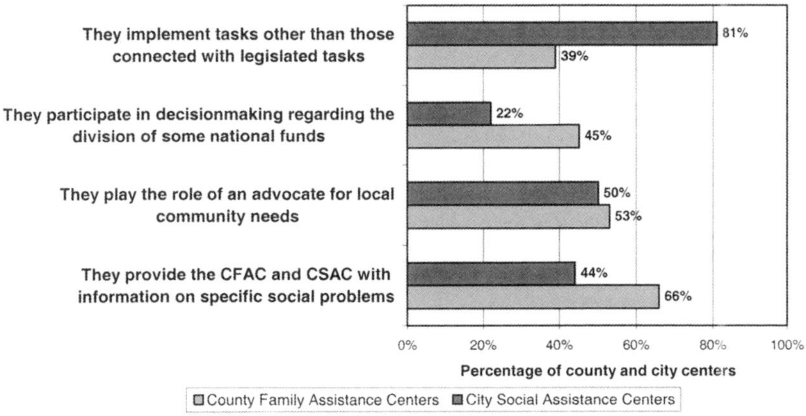

Figure 9. Other roles of social service NGOs in the context of cooperation with county and city family assistance centers, July, 2000

Indeed, it appears the introduction of county family assistance centers has facilitated new unmandated linkages not only between state and society (county-NGO cooperation) but also between different levels of government (county-municipality cooperation). A study conducted at the Academy of Economics in Poznań supports this finding of new linkages. A survey of regular counties showed that the majority in general (not just in the area of social services) declared close cooperation with other local entities including municipalities and NGOs.[57] Given the preceding discussion, the author's hypothesis that the reform would have little influence on civil society in the area of social services is largely unconfirmed.

Policy on Development and Use of a County Strategy. Another goal of the reform was to improve the societal control or monitoring of public activities. While one of the main routes to achieving this goal is through local elections, other institutions put in place with the reform worked to serve this same goal. In the area of social services county-level centers are required to use a needs assessment and goal planning instrument that introduces a feedback mechanism for county and other officials. This "county strategy for solving social problems" by design is to be developed with the help of the local community, especially in assessing county social service needs. It is then to be used in the centers themselves, in elected county councils, by county officials and administrators, and

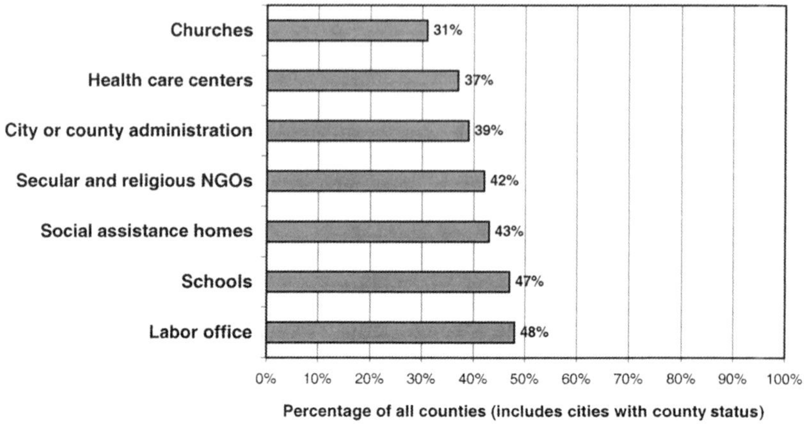

Figure 10. Participation of local institutions in the development of the county strategy for solving social problems in all counties, July, 2000

even on the regional level in planning sessions that address how to meet county needs. The survey first determined to what degree this instrument had been developed by county and city centers and how involved local institutions were in that process. It then asked directors to indicate where the strategy had been made use of thus far. The survey found that half of both county and city centers had a complete county strategy in place and 35 percent said they had one partially completed.[58] About half of counties and cities indicated the involvement of NGOs, social assistance homes, schools, and county labor offices in the needs assessment aspect of it. Thirty to forty percent claimed the participation of churches, health care centers, and the county or city administration (see figure 10).[59] These figures provide an encouraging sign that where county strategies are being developed, local institutions are involved.

Use of the "county strategy for solving social problems" as a societal oversight instrument is, however, only effective as far as it is actually used by public decision-making entities. The survey found that half of all county and city centers were using the county strategy during their own planning activities (which correlates with the half that have a completed strategy). About 35 percent said the strategy was used in the county or city elected council and administration and one-fifth indicated it was used by the president of the county or city. Only 3 percent indicated a strategy existed but was not being used (see figure 11). While use of the strategy in

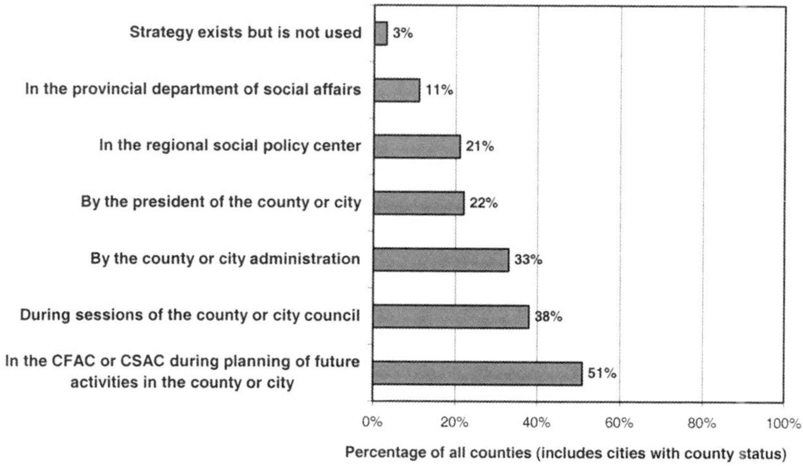

Figure 11. Use of the "county strategy for solving social problems" in all counties, July, 2000

the county and city family assistance center is fairly high (in comparison to the number of completed or partially completed strategies) there is clearly room for growth in its use in forums that have more widespread influence on program development and finance. Nonetheless, these findings indicate a promising start for an area of social policy that is working to achieve a wider reform goal of societal oversight. The author's hypothesis that societal control over social services would be minimal is partially accurate given the presence of only one mechanism that was being used in only half of the counties. Nonetheless, where the county strategy for solving social problems was being used effectively there is hope that some oversight by the local community is occurring.

Policy on Services Decentralized to County Centers. One of the goals of reformers was that by decentralizing services there would be less physical distance between where recipients lived and the service itself. Less distance would mean greater efficiency in use of that service for the recipient and, in the case of some social services where home visits are made and area needs assessments done, greater efficiency in the administration's provision of the service. Three services that were highly developed on the provincial level, decentralized to the county level, and almost fully implemented included: referral services to social assistance homes, foster care services, and services for the disabled.[60] County and city directors were asked if the distance to each of these services for recipients was less, the same, or greater after the reform. On average, two-thirds of the directors indicated the distance was less after the reform with one quarter indicating it had remained the same. Indeed, other studies also indicate that overall accessibility improved for these services after the reform.[61]

This chapter shows that compromised policy resulted in outcomes that were contrary to original reform goals and that reform goals even within a specific policy area, at times, work at cross purposes with other goals of the reform. Without sufficient fiscal decentralization (meaning here local revenue-generating authority and funds over which there is local revenue assignment authority), expected improvements to democracy through the path of local elections were not found. Moreover, implementation of the reform was put in jeopardy when continuing fiscal centralization did not provide sufficient funds for decentralized responsibilities. Overarching reform policy also resulted inadvertently in disparities in some social services between regular counties and cities with county status. Decentralization did bring some services much closer to recipients. Service-specific policy that met reform goals on the surface, such as decentralization of social assistance homes and disability eligibility offices and the hiring of county and city center directors by the county head, worked against goals in other areas such as administrative efficiency and to some extent professionalization of the civil service.

What this chapter also shows is that despite the many difficulties with reform development and implementation, the reform resulted in some outcomes that were important to a postcommunist country in particular. In Poland, where civil society activities are still much lower than in Western countries, the addition of new public institutions on the local level has been an important step in encouraging the growth of civil society—an important aspect of democracy. Research results show that new county family assistance centers are beginning to draw in, work with, and support the community (including nongovernmental organizations) in ways that were not occurring before the reform. The flow of information and cooperation between municipal and county centers is itself indicative of the self-initiative many of these new county centers are exhibiting.

Involvement of the community in needs assessment and programming can also mean increased efficiency as services begin to reflect local needs. Thus, while the reform resulted in some outcomes that were not in harmony with original goals, other outcomes, mostly stemming from what was *added* to the system, indicate that some important goals of the reform are starting to be met.

6 Conclusion
A Synthesis of Politics and Outcomes

Decentralizing Poland involved an array of actors and ideas interacting in a political and administrative framework that all worked to shape reform outcomes in particular ways. Closer examination of the politics of the 1999 public administration reform reveals that certain patterns of political behavior resulted in specific policy outcomes for citizens. Though particular to this decentralization reform in Poland, this chapter introduces a model for types of decentralization politics and corresponding policy outcomes. The model illustrates how, due to the politics of reform, prescribed policy goals of reform initiators were compromised. Compromise, more often than not, favored the expansion of local-level democracy over efficiency. Indeed, assessing decentralization reforms in Poland reveals that a country can have very specific ideas about decentralization even given international influences. In the case of Poland these preferences were shaped by policy actors that are still grappling with how much democracy to let into the policy process.

A Model for Decentralization Politics and Policy Outcomes

The particular political environment in which decentralization policy was generated in Poland resulted in several types of politics that corresponded to the different kinds of policy outcomes outlined in the previous chapter. Exclusionary politics of neoliberals resulted in deviant policy. Contested politics, best explained by disjointed pluralism, resulted in counterproductive policy. Largely uncontested but uninformed politics also had the outcome of counterproductive policy. Finally, uncontested politics resulted in more-or-less expected policy (see table 4). This model is based on the perspective of reform initiators, so while they would view policy outcomes as deviant or counterproductive, other actors (such as neoliberals or interest groups) may view the very same outcomes as positive. The political structure and policy process found in Poland provided the means by which their ideas were accommodated. Decentralization outcomes, therefore, reflect to some extent the understanding and

Table 4. Types of Politics and Corresponding Policy Outcomes for Decentralization in Poland

Type of Politics	Exclusionary	Contested	Uncontested-Uninformed	Uncontested
	↓	↓	↓	↓
Policy Outcome	Deviant	Counterproductive	Counterproductive	Expected

preferences for decentralization of a broader group of Poles than just reform initiators.

The model of politics and corresponding policy outcomes was created on the basis of inductive observation of the study's empirical data informed by political theory. Its purpose is to show general trends in politics and outcomes for this particular decentralization reform in its specific political context. Though the model is therefore not intended as a theory, it can be viewed as a theoretical proposition to be investigated by future comparative studies of postcommunist countries. Factors that may limit the ability to generalize from the Polish case to other postcommunist states include its then status as a first-wave country for accession to the European Union, its relatively homogenous make-up (it lacks a sizable ethnic minority), and the fact that its public administration reform was more far-reaching in breadth and depth than in other postcommunist countries. The following is a description of each of the model's categories for type of politics and corresponding policy outcome.

Exclusionary politics is where policymakers limit the participation of other groups in the policymaking process in order to achieve policy outcomes they have prescribed. According to Haggard and Kaufman this narrow approach to policymaking may interfere with the actual undertaking of a reform initiative.[1] The practice of this type of politics in Poland was part of the reason why fiscal decentralization stalled, which necessitated a substitute reform that deviated from the original reform goal. In addition, self-isolating policymakers were in a position to manipulate this substitute reform to their own ends, resulting in another deviant policy. Deviant policy here is policy that did not achieve original reform goals. Contested politics are those where coalitions promoting different interests force compromise that moves policy in unintended directions. This type of politics is informed by Schickler's theory of disjointed pluralism, which shows how tensions and interactions of different interest coalitions in legislative politics can result in unstable and contradictory institutions. Here, such policy outcomes were labeled "counterproductive" in the sense that though they may have addressed a goal of the reform they worked at cross purposes with other goals.

Uncontested-uninformed politics are politics where, though minor conflict is present, majority opinion moves reform in the direction originally intended by reformers with little or no compromise to the basic premise of the reform. However, policymakers themselves are uninformed about possible negative consequences of larger reform on specific policy or about how to create the best policy for a particular policy area. This type of politics is informed by the literatures on the cognitive limitations of policymakers and the specific policymaking environment found in transitioning countries. It also results in counterproductive policy as defined above. Uncontested politics are those where conflict between competing interests is minimal, which precludes the need for compromise, and where policymakers are relatively informed or are not informed entirely but their gamble with the policy they initiate pays off.[2] With the Polish reform, the result of such politics was expected policy, understood as policy that shows progress in reaching goals and does not conflict with other goals of the reform. The following section reviews the specific politics that led to particular policy outcomes in the area of social services with the decentralization reform in Poland.[3]

Exclusionary Politics and Deviant Policy

Exclusionary politics were found in the neoliberal isolationist approach to policymaking that characterized reform development for fiscal decentralization. The neoliberal Undersecretary of State for Fiscal Decentralization Jerzy Miller, successfully blocked the involvement of representatives of local government and other government officials in the development of fiscal policy for the reform. Failure to involve others resulted in a fiscal decentralization project that found little support outside Miller's small circle. As a result of this and other factors, fiscal decentralization was put on hold for the first two years of the reform, which necessitated the need for a temporary centralized plan for funding subnational governments. Miller, using the same isolationist approach in developing the temporary plan, was able to use manipulation and misinformation to transfer fewer funds to programs that had been decentralized with the reform. Exclusionary tactics thus contributed to policy that directly deviated from original reform goals: fiscal policy remained centralized and adequate funds were not provided for administratively decentralized services. Moreover, this situation seriously limited the democratic functioning of new county and provincial elected governments, another goal of the reform.

In the area of social services lack of fiscal decentralization and underfunding most profoundly affected county services administered by new county family assistance centers. Social services that were given to counties as their administrative and financial responsibility were drastically underfunded, because lack of fiscal decentralization meant that counties did not have enough of their own revenue to fund such services. This situation also meant that elected officials, and thus citizens through them, did not have a say in how funding was spent on county social services.

Contested Politics and Counterproductive Policy

Contested politics were found especially in reform development regarding the territorial division of the state and administrative decentralization. Specifically, the number of counties was determined in a compromise between reformers and county interest groups where reformers gained support for the overall reform in exchange for increasing the number of counties well past a number that would provide an administratively efficient system. Likewise, the number of cities with county status was a negotiated compromise between reformers and interest groups defending old provincial capitals. Reformers received support for a reduced number of provinces (and a reduced number of provincial capitals) in exchange for extending "city with county status" to many of the old provincial capitals. Also, in terms of administrative decentralization, reformers had to compromise with central ministries on the number of functions passed down to subnational units or be faced with lack of ministerial support for the overall reform. Policy outcomes of such contested politics proved to be counterproductive. That is, decentralization that improved democracy did take place but most often at the cost of administrative efficiency, another goal of the reform.

Contested politics affected social service outcomes in a number of ways. The most immediate effect was disparity in county social services between urban and more rural areas. The large number of cities with county status meant that most of the major urban areas were able to draw on county *and* rich municipal funds to cover the costs of county social services, while regular counties in less urban areas had only county reserves to draw on. Also, the large number of small counties is already posing an economy of scale problem for some social services where the county level is now too small to operate those services for the few beneficiaries found there. Such programs include disability eligibility offices, crisis intervention centers, specialized counseling, and juvenile rehabilitation centers. Efforts at cross-county cooperation to correct the situation have been minimal. In terms of administrative decentralization of social services, unlike other policy areas, the Ministry of Labor and Social Policy gave less resistance than other central ministries to the decentralization of social welfare functions and saw many social services transferred to lower levels with the reform.[4]

Uncontested-Uninformed Politics and Counterproductive Policy

Uncontested-uninformed politics were also found in reforms to the territorial division of the state and administrative decentralization. One of the main goals of the reform was to drastically reduce the number of provinces to bring Poland's regions in line with those in Western European countries. While politics concerning the specific number of fewer provinces (ranging from twelve to sixteen) to be implemented were of the contested type, the basic goal of the overall reduction in provinces was achieved without compromise (there had been proposals for twenty-five provinces and for maintaining the existing forty-nine provinces). Reformers, however, were unaware that the introduction of a much smaller number of provinces had unintended consequences for intergovernmental relationships between central government offices that continued to be maintained on the provincial level and municipalities. In terms of administrative decentralization, some service areas were decentralized with little resistance and, therefore, need for compromise. Here, however, uninformed policymakers struggled with how best to create policy. In both cases, counterproductive policy resulted where goals of efficiency were undermined.

This type of politics was reflected in social service outcomes in several ways. With the reduction of provinces to sixteen, provincial departments of social affairs (under the jurisdiction of the central government) were in effect centralized in relation to municipal social assistance centers. As a result, social service workers on the municipal level had a much more difficult time communicating with these provincial offices when difficulties or questions arose. Some policy specific to social services, though meeting goals of bringing government and services closer to the people, failed in other ways with respect to efficiency. For example, policy allowing for directors of county family assistance centers to be hired by the county head stood at cross-purposes with the goal of developing a professional civil service. Also, the decentralization of social assistance homes to the county level created a series of problems in funding and access because homes were not spread evenly across counties.

Uncontested Politics and Expected Policy

Some of the politics involving political and administrative decentralization were identified as uncontested politics. For example, the establishment of county self-government and the decentralization of some functions fall into this category. Expected policy was found here with some services that were decentralized and did bring services closer to recipients without interfering with other goals of the reform. Some of the goals reformers set, however, had no specific politics of their own because they were expected consequences of implementing other aspects of the reform. Victories, where they were found, in political and administrative decentralization laid the groundwork for the success of these intended side effects. Two such expected consequences found as expected policy were the stimulation of civil society on the local level and increased societal control and monitoring over services.

In the area of social services, expected policy was found that met reform goals but did not conflict with other goals. The decentralization of some services did indeed bring services closer to citizens without any apparent negative consequences. These include referral services to social assistance homes, foster care services, and services for the disabled (excluding disability eligibility offices). Also, civil society appeared to be supported by the introduction of county family assistance centers. Important here was their non-mandated cooperation with municipal social assistance centers and nongovernmental organizations. Increased societal control or monitoring over services also appeared to be taking place in social services on the county level, though not through the path of local elections. Here, the development and use of a county strategy to address social problems showed promising signs of community feedback that is integrated into planning sessions for county services.

Culture and Value Judgments

This study has examined decentralization politics and outcomes for democracy and efficiency by analyzing social service decentralization in the context of postcommunist Poland. Necessarily, decentralization policy was analyzed relative to the starting point for decentralization in Poland: against a backdrop of values and institutions created as a result of communist centralization, against the wider Western European community, and in the context of a new, transitioning democracy. Polish ideas about decentralization were manifest through the goals reform initiators had for decentralization as well as through those who contested or opposed these goals.

Common practice in the study of decentralization outcomes, however, is to measure success or failure against standards for decentralization adhered to by the given researcher or research community. Indeed, Western advocates for or against decentralization and its ability to improve democracy and efficiency could provide starkly different evaluations of Poland's decentralization goals and outcomes because they assign different value to levels and kinds of democracy and efficiency. Such an approach provides little in the way of constructive and useful feedback for societies that are operating from a completely different set of values and starting point regarding decentralization. Paul Appleby raised this issue about administrative arrangements that international researchers are only now beginning to re-learn. He states, "Efficiency in one society is not efficiency in another.... The spirit in which a governmental organization is conducted is largely in response to the values and mores of the society."[5]

Indeed, decisions about democracy, efficiency, and the "proper" balance between the two are ultimately value judgments.[6] How one views and evaluates the goals and results of decentralization is actually a subjective determination often colored by one's own experiences and particular starting point for decentralization. International organizations involved in providing practical, technical advice to a host of different governments have recently begun to note these differences in preferences across countries though they do not always account for the wider politics of decentralization. In the context of decentralization in East Central Europe, Urban Institute experts (writing for the U.S. Agency for International Development and the World Bank) note that "[cultural values] have to do with subjective considerations of what is fair or just. Countries that place a high value on ensuring universal access to certain services, such as education, may be less inclined to decentralize those services than other countries that place higher value on local choice or control."[7] The World Bank also identified this as an important factor in their work on decentralization in developing countries: "Decentralization has been likened to a soufflé where all ingredients must be present in the right amounts and prepared in the right way to achieve success. Moreover, like a soufflé, the best method of preparation will depend on the environment and the best mix of ingredients is a matter of taste."[8]

While work on decentralization in international consulting projects has begun to include the "cultural preference" factor, it is largely missing in studies and evaluations of decentralization outcomes. Analysis of decentralization has, rather, taken the form of measuring success or failure against the researcher's pre-conceived idea of what that entails, usually involving a predominant emphasis on Western ideas of efficiency. Rather than apply some foreign measure of what decentralization "should" have been (which itself would have been contested), this study analyzed and evaluated decentralization in the Polish context against Polish expectations for reform. Thus, it not only evaluated reform outcomes against initial Polish goals for the reform but also analyzed how Polish politics skewed outcomes and often undermined those goals though they accommodated other preferences found in Polish society. Indeed, a main result of the study was that it showed how cultural and societal factors manifest themselves through the democratic process and were ultimately reflected in reform outcomes. Hence, there was a focus on not only ideologies and historical and international factors that influence reform but also political mechanisms in analyzing reform outcomes.

Refining Schickler's Theory of Disjointed Pluralism

This study has shown that Schickler's theory of disjointed pluralism, while useful in explaining many aspects of the reform, was unable to account for the exclusionary politics that brought deviant outcomes or the uncontested politics that resulted in expected outcomes. Disjointed pluralism also had to be framed in the particular political system found in Poland. The exclusionary politics of neoliberals are a hallmark of the transition environment found in many postcommunist countries. Greskovits, citing reform in East Central Europe and South America, refers to this as the "neoliberal transformation strategy" characterized by the "exclusionary features" of new democracies, "not only with respect to economic policy making, but for many important political issues."[9] Schickler's theory was limited on this account because it was formulated on the basis of a fully consolidated democracy. Application to a transitioning democracy, Poland, revealed that it cannot account for the exclusionary politics often found in the transition setting.

The finding of uncontested politics that resulted in expected policy can most likely be attributed to the different types of reform policies examined in this study in contrast to Schickler's narrow focus on reform of legislative institutions. As Kingdon shows, different policy types can attract different levels of involvement by a host of different policy actors at a given point in time and thus by extension generate more or less conflict during policy formation.[10] Reform of legislative institutions, as Schickler clearly demonstrates, has been fraught with conflict throughout the history of the U.S. Congress, due to its direct attack on disparate vested interests of congressmen. This study provides evidence, however, that when different policies are examined the existence of conflict that necessitates compromise depends on the policy in question. This as yet theoretical proposition awaits future applications of disjointed pluralism to the study of other policy.

Applying Schickler's theory of disjointed pluralism also required framing the theory in the context of the political system particular to Poland. Poland's pattern of veto points structures political power and behavior in certain ways that make the policy process different than the process in the United States. The compromises of the public administration reform explained by disjointed pluralism were at times structured by the veto points in the Polish political system. At times, veto points opened the door to situations that ultimately required compromise, whereas in a different political context need for compromise would not have arisen. More opportunities for compromise meant more opportunities for those against reform to shape reform outcomes in unexpected ways. This study demonstrates that application of the theory of disjointed pluralism in countries outside the United States needs to be supplemented by a discussion of how a country's political system structures opportunities for compromise.

Though not its main purpose, this book addresses a debate in East Central European studies on whether Western democratic theory can be used to examine political processes in transitioning countries. Though some few additions were made to the theory of disjointed pluralism to account for all Polish reform politics, this study shows that Western democratic theory is applicable in a postcommunist context. Specifically, this research has demonstrated that the study of democracy in Western and postcommunist transitioning countries is not mutually exclusive.

Future Directions for Research

Research building on the work presented here could proceed in a number of directions. First, the theoretical framework for understanding the politics of decentralization (presented in chapter 3) would be strengthened by its successful application to the politics of decentralization in other postcommunist countries. Second, the model for types of decentralization politics and corresponding policy outcomes can be tested and refined into a theoretical model also through its application to decentralization reform in other transitioning countries. Third, the model can be revised to look at reform outcomes from the perspective of other actors (especially those opposing reform) or approach reform outcomes from a neutral perspective. Finally, as suggested, the finding that the theory of disjointed pluralism may not be useful in assessing the politics of certain types of policy can be substantiated through examination of the politics of different types of policy.

Democracy and Decentralization in Poland

The success of major decentralization reforms in a postcommunist, democratic context, when studied from goal through policy design and implementation, was found in this study to be far more determined by the politics of national-level democracy than by prescriptions of policy experts. While goals may reflect desired outcomes anticipated by policymakers, realization of them is subject to the realities of conflicting interests and limited resources, technical and financial. Indeed, though goals of decentralization in Poland called for the improvement of both democracy and efficiency it is interesting to find that outcomes indicate reformers were more likely to advance the goal of democratization over the goal of efficiency when the two came in conflict. Efficiency was also at times undermined due to uninformed policymaking.

Analysis of the public administration reform has also provided an interesting commentary on the functioning of democratic governance in Poland. On the one end are neoliberals who seek to limit involvement in policymaking with the justification that they know what is best for all. On the other end are politicians who allow the preferences of citizens to determine policy far beyond reformers' initial ideas of what is in the best interest for all. Thus, the question of how much democracy to allow into the policymaking process is an issue Polish lawmakers still appear to be grappling with. Meanwhile, the results of these extreme approaches are being reflected in policy outcomes.

Overall, this analysis has shown that improving democracy and efficiency on subnational levels through national-level democracy can be elusive. Scholars of decentralization agree that it takes a host of factors working together for prescribed outcomes of democracy and efficiency to be achieved. Speaking broadly, two East Central European scholars note, "The development of local and regional democracy ... needs to be seen as a process, with its gradual achievement depending on the interaction of a number of factors."[11] What is often overlooked are the politics of reform, which can prevent these factors from coming together in expected ways or even materializing at all.

APPENDIX A

The Constitution of the Republic of Poland, April 2, 1997 (*excerpts*)

Chapter I. The Republic

Article 3

The Republic of Poland shall be a unitary State.

Article 15

1 The territorial system of the Republic of Poland shall ensure the decentralization of public power.

2 The basic territorial division of the State shall be determined by statute, allowing for the social, economic and cultural ties which ensure to the territorial units the capacity to perform their public duties.

Article 16

1 The inhabitants of the units of basic territorial division shall form a self-governing community in accordance with law.

2 Local self-government shall participate in the exercise of public power. The substantial part of public duties which local self-government is empowered to discharge by statute shall be done in its own name and under its own responsibility.

Chapter VII. Local Self-Government

Article 163

Local self-government shall perform public tasks not reserved by the Constitution or statutes to the organs of other public authorities.

Article 164

1 The commune *(gmina)* shall be the basic unit of local self-government.

2 Other units of regional and/or local self-government shall be specified by statute.

3 The commune shall perform all tasks of local self-government not reserved to other units of local self-government.

Article 165

1 Units of local self-government shall possess legal personality. They shall have rights of ownership and other property rights.

2 The self-governing nature of units of local self-government shall be protected by the courts.

Article 166

1 Public duties aimed at satisfying the needs of a self-governing community shall be performed by units of local self-government as their direct responsibility.

2 If the fundamental needs of the State shall so require, a statute may instruct units of local self-government to perform other public duties. The mode of transfer and manner of performance of the duties so allocated shall be specified by statute.

3 The administrative courts shall settle jurisdictional disputes between units of local self-government and units of government administration.

Article 167

1 Units of local self-government shall be assured public funds adequate for the performance of the duties assigned to them.

2 The revenues of units of local self-government shall consist of their own revenues as well as general subsidies and specific grants from the State Budget.

3 The sources of revenues for units of local self-government shall be specified by statute.

4 Alterations to the scope of duties and authorities of units of local self-government shall be made in conjunction with appropriate alterations to their share of public revenues.

Article 168

To the extent established by statute, units of local self-government shall have the right to set the level of local taxes and charges.

Article 169

1 Units of local self-government shall perform their duties through constitutive and executive organs.

2 Elections to constitutive organs shall be universal, direct, equal and shall be conducted by secret ballot. The principles

and procedures for submitting candidates and for the conduct of elections, as well as the requirements for the validity of elections, shall be specified by statute.

3 The principles and procedures for the election and dismissal of executive organs of units of local self-government shall be specified by statute.

4 The internal organizational structure of units of local self-government shall be specified, within statutory limits, by their constitutive organs.

Article 170

Members of a self-governing community may decide, by means of a referendum, matters concerning their community, including the dismissal of an organ of local self-government established by direct election. The principles of and procedures for conducting a local referendum shall be specified by statute.

Article 171

1 The legality of actions by a local self-government shall be subject to review.

2 The organs exercising review over the activity of units of local self-government shall be: the Prime Minister and voivodes and regarding financial matters–regional audit chambers.

3 On a motion of the Prime Minister, the Sejm may dissolve a constitutive organ of local self-government if it has flagrantly violated the Constitution or a statute.

Article 172

1 Units of local self-government shall have the right to associate.

2 A unit of local self-government shall have the right to join international associations of local and regional communities as well as cooperate with local and regional communities of other states.

3 The principles governing the exercise of the rights referred to in paras. 1 and 2 above by units of local self-government shall be specified by statute.

APPENDIX B

European Charter of Local Self-Government (*excerpt*)

Strasbourg, 15.X.1985

Preamble

The member States of the Council of Europe, signatory hereto,

Considering that the aim of the Council of Europe is to achieve a greater unity between its members for the purpose of safeguarding and realising the ideals and principles which are their common heritage;

Considering that one of the methods by which this aim is to be achieved is through agreements in the administrative field;

Considering that the local authorities are one of the main foundations of any democratic regime;

Considering that the right of citizens to participate in the conduct of public affairs is one of the democratic principles that are shared by all member States of the Council of Europe;

Considering that it is at local level that this right can be most directly exercised;

Convinced that the existence of local authorities with real responsibilities can provide an administration which is both effective and close to the citizen;

Aware that the safeguarding and reinforcement of local self-government in the different European countries is an important contribution to the construction of a Europe based on the principles of democracy and the decentralisation of power;

Asserting that this entails the existence of local authorities endowed with democratically constituted decision-making bodies and possessing a wide degree of autonomy with regard to their responsibilities, the ways and means by which those responsibilities are exercised and the resources required for their fulfillment,

Have agreed as follows:

Article 1

The Parties undertake to consider themselves bound by the following articles in the manner and to the extent prescribed in Article 12 of this Charter.

Part I

Article 2—Constitutional and legal foundation for local self-government

The principle of local self-government shall be recognised in domestic legislation, and where practicable in the constitution.

Article 3—Concept of local self-government

1 Local self-government denotes the right and the ability of local authorities, within the limits of the law, to regulate and manage a substantial share of public affairs under their own responsibility and in the interests of the local population.

2 This right shall be exercised by councils or assemblies composed of members freely elected by secret ballot on the basis of direct, equal, universal suffrage, and which may possess executive organs responsible to them. This provision shall in no way affect recourse to assemblies of citizens, referendums or any other form of direct citizen participation where it is permitted by statute.

Article 4—Scope of local self-government

1 The basic powers and responsibilities of local authorities shall be prescribed by the constitution or by statute. However, this provision shall not prevent the attribution to local authorities of powers and responsibilities for specific purposes in accordance with the law.

2 Local authorities shall, within the limits of the law, have full discretion to exercise their initiative with regard to any matter which is not excluded from their competence nor assigned to any other authority.

3 Public responsibilities shall generally be exercised, in preference, by those authorities which are closest to the citizen. Allocation of responsibility to another authority should weigh up the extent and nature of the task and requirements of efficiency and economy.

4 Powers given to local authorities shall normally be full and exclusive. They may not be undermined or limited by another, central or regional, authority except as provided for by the law.

5 Where powers are delegated to them by a central or regional authority, local authorities shall, insofar as possible, be allowed discretion in adapting their exercise to local conditions.

6 Local authorities shall be consulted, insofar as possible, in due time and in an appropriate way in the planning and decision-making processes for all matters which concern them directly.

Article 5—Protection of local authority boundaries

Changes in local authority boundaries shall not be made without prior consultation of the local communities concerned, possibly by means of a referendum where this is permitted by statute.

Article 6—Appropriate administrative structures and resources for the tasks of local authorities

1 Without prejudice to more general statutory provisions, local authorities shall be able to determine their own internal administrative structures in order to adapt them to local needs and ensure effective management.

2 The conditions of service of local government employees shall be such as to permit the recruitment of high-quality staff on the basis of merit and competence; to this end adequate training opportunities, remuneration and career prospects shall be provided.

Article 7—Conditions under which responsibilities at local level are exercised

1 The conditions of office of local elected representatives shall provide for free exercise of their functions.

2 They shall allow for appropriate financial compensation for expenses incurred in the exercise of the office in question as well as, where appropriate, compensation for loss of earnings or remuneration for work done and corresponding social welfare protection.

3 Any functions and activities which are deemed incompatible with the holding of local elective office shall be determined by statute or fundamental legal principles.

Article 8—Administrative supervision of local authorities' activities

1 Any administrative supervision of local authorities may only be exercised according to such procedures and in such cases as are provided for by the constitution or by statute.

2 Any administrative supervision of the activities of the local authorities shall normally aim only at ensuring compliance with the law and with constitutional principles. Administrative supervision may however be exercised with regard to expediency by higher-level authorities in respect of tasks the execution of which is delegated to local authorities.

3 Administrative supervision of local authorities shall be exercised in such a way as to ensure that the intervention of the controlling authority is kept in proportion to the importance of the interests which it is intended to protect.

Article 9—Financial resources of local authorities

1 Local authorities shall be entitled, within national economic policy, to adequate financial resources of their own, of which they may dispose freely within the framework of their powers.

2 Local authorities' financial resources shall be commensurate with the responsibilities provided for by the constitution and the law.

3 Part at least of the financial resources of local authorities shall derive from local taxes and charges of which, within the limits of statute, they have the power to determine the rate.

4 The financial systems on which resources available to local authorities are based shall be of a sufficiently diversified and buoyant nature to enable them to keep pace as far as practically possible with the real evolution of the cost of carrying out their tasks.

5 The protection of financially weaker local authorities calls for the institution of financial equalisation procedures or equivalent measures which are designed to correct the effects of the unequal distribution of potential sources of finance and of the financial burden they must support. Such procedures or measures shall not diminish the discretion local authorities may exercise within their own sphere of responsibility.

6 Local authorities shall be consulted, in an appropriate manner, on the way in which redistributed resources are to be allocated to them.

7 As far as possible, grants to local authorities shall not be earmarked for the financing of specific projects. The provision of grants shall not remove the basic freedom of local authorities to exercise policy discretion within their own jurisdiction.

8 For the purpose of borrowing for capital investment, local authorities shall have access to the national capital market within the limits of the law.

Article 10—Local authorities' right to associate

1 Local authorities shall be entitled, in exercising their powers, to co-operate and, within the framework of the law, to form consortia with other local authorities in order to carry out tasks of common interest.

2 The entitlement of local authorities to belong to an association for the protection and promotion of their common interests and to belong to an international association of local authorities shall be recognised in each State.

3 Local authorities shall be entitled, under such conditions as may be provided for by the law, to co-operate with their counterparts in other States.

Article 11—Legal protection of local self-government

Local authorities shall have the right of recourse to a judicial remedy in order to secure free exercise of their powers and respect for such principles of local self-government as are enshrined in the constitution or domestic legislation.

APPENDIX C

Survey Instrument

English Translation of the County Survey

The first document in this appendix is a translation of the county survey that was written originally in Polish. Some of the translated English words and phrases may not appear to be the best choice for survey use in English; their Polish equivalents, however, were appropriate. The formatting has been altered to accommodate the margins of the book format. The original survey was nine pages long. Explanatory comments found in brackets [ ] were not part of the original Polish survey.

Survey—Director of the County Family Assistance Center (CFAC)

REGULAR AND SUBURBAN COUNTIES

County ____________________________ Voivodship ______________
Interviewer _________________________ Date ____________________
Date the CFAC was established _________________________________

This research is the result of collaboration between a research group from the Center for Self-Government and Local Development of the University of Warsaw, the Association of Polish Counties, and a doctoral student from Syracuse University, USA. The goal of the study is a better understanding of the state of social welfare after the 1999 administrative reform. The Social Research Workshop in Sopot will conduct the research in 99 randomly chosen counties in Poland. This is a sociological study and as such obtained responses will be handled according to the principle of complete anonymity. This means that no one besides the interviewer will know your responses. Participation in the study is voluntary.

We thank you for your cooperation!
Please mark your answers with an X.

1. A) **Please describe the degree to which the tasks below have been realized in your county:** (please choose one of these answers)	1. B) If tasks were not realized or partially realized, what were the *main reasons* for this? (please choose no more than *two* of these answers)

		Realized	**Partly realized**	**Not realized**	**There are no clients in this category**	**Another institution realizes the task**	Lack of financial resources	Sufficient resources, but lack of appropriate building space	Sufficient resources, but lack of educated people to hire	Appropriate personnel, but lack of training—need for new skills	Ambiguous regulations	Other main reason that does not appear here
1.1	Referral of people to social assistance homes.	**0**	**1**	**2**	**3**	**4**	0	1	2	3	4	5
1.2	Provision of information regarding laws and rights.	**0**	**1**	**2**	**3**	**4**	0	1	2	3	4	5
1.3	Organization of specialized counseling.	**0**	**1**	**2**	**3**	**4**	0	1	2	3	4	5
1.4	Development of a county strategy for solving social problems.	**0**	**1**	**2**	**3**	**4**	0	1	2	3	4	5
1.5	Management of a crisis intervention center.	**0**	**1**	**2**	**3**	**4**	0	1	2	3	4	5
1.6	Assuring the training and professional improvement of the social service staff.	**0**	**1**	**2**	**3**	**4**	0	1	2	3	4	5
1.7	Case consultation with Municipal Social Assistance Centers.	**0**	**1**	**2**	**3**	**4**	0	1	2	3	4	5
1.8	Financing county support centers (except those for the mentally ill).	**0**	**1**	**2**	**3**	**4**	0	1	2	3	4	5
1.9	Assistance with integration for those leaving juvenile delinquent centers, institutions for minors, and foster families.	**0**	**1**	**2**	**3**	**4**	0	1	2	3	4	5
1.10	Organizing and managing juvenile delinquent centers.	**0**	**1**	**2**	**3**	**4**	0	1	2	3	4	5
1.11	Organizing and assuring county support centers for the mentally ill.	**0**	**1**	**2**	**3**	**4**	0	1	2	3	4	5
1.12	Provision of monetary assistance for people leaving various kinds of juvenile delinquent centers, institutions for minors, and foster families.	**0**	**1**	**2**	**3**	**4**	0	1	2	3	4	5
1.13	Organizing care in foster families.	**0**	**1**	**2**	**3**	**4**	0	1	2	3	4	5
1.14	Provision of monetary assistance to partly cover the cost of children in foster families.	**0**	**1**	**2**	**3**	**4**	0	1	2	3	4	5
1.15	Assistance for refugees.	**0**	**1**	**2**	**3**	**4**	0	1	2	3	4	5
1.16	Assuring resources for payment of workers realizing central government tasks in the county.	**0**	**1**	**2**	**3**	**4**	0	1	2	3	4	5
1.17	Realization of tasks from the National Fund for Rehabilitation of the Disabled (NFRD).	**0**	**1**	**2**	**3**	**4**	0	1	2	3	4	5

2) According to you, to what degree did central and local government funds cover need in the area of the following tasks?* * without transfers from other local government units other than your own county.	1999					January 1, 2000 to June 15, 2000				
	0%	**25%**	**50%**	**75%**	**100%**	0%	25%	50%	75%	100%
2.1 Organizing specialized counseling.	**0**	**1**	**2**	**3**	**4**	0	1	2	3	4
2.2 Assuring services in social assistance homes (if there are such homes in the county).	**0**	**1**	**2**	**3**	**4**	0	1	2	3	4
2.3 Development of a county strategy for solving social problems.	**0**	**1**	**2**	**3**	**4**	0	1	2	3	4
2.4 Management of a crisis intervention center.	**0**	**1**	**2**	**3**	**4**	0	1	2	3	4
2.5 Assuring the training and professional improvement of the social service staff.	**0**	**1**	**2**	**3**	**4**	0	1	2	3	4
2.6 Case consultation with Municipal Social Assistance Centers.	**0**	**1**	**2**	**3**	**4**	0	1	2	3	4
2.7 Financing county support centers (except those for the mentally ill).	**0**	**1**	**2**	**3**	**4**	0	1	2	3	4
2.8 Assistance with integration for those leaving various kinds of juvenile delinquent centers, institutions for minors, and foster families.	**0**	**1**	**2**	**3**	**4**	0	1	2	3	4
2.9 Organizing and managing juvenile delinquent centers.	**0**	**1**	**2**	**3**	**4**	0	1	2	3	4
2.10 Organizing and assuring county support centers for the mentally ill.	**0**	**1**	**2**	**3**	**4**	0	1	2	3	4
2.11 Provision of monetary resources for people leaving various kinds of juvenile delinquent centers, institutions for minors, and foster families.	**0**	**1**	**2**	**3**	**4**	0	1	2	3	4
2.12 Provision of monetary assistance to partly cover the costs of children in foster families.	**0**	**1**	**2**	**3**	**4**	0	1	2	3	4
2.13 Assistance for refugees.	**0**	**1**	**2**	**3**	**4**	0	1	2	3	4
2.14 Assuring resources for payment of workers realizing central government tasks in the county.	**0**	**1**	**2**	**3**	**4**	0	1	2	3	4
2.15 Realization of tasks from the National Fund for Rehabilitation of the Disabled (NFRD).	**0**	**1**	**2**	**3**	**4**	0	1	2	3	4

3) In a case of lack of resources, did your CFAC make use of the following solutions?
(please mark all appropriate answers on the line)

_____ 1 use of voivodship reserves
_____ 2 use of county reserves
_____ 3 use of funds assigned to tasks commissioned to the county [by the central government in order to realize county tasks]
_____ 4 cooperation with other counties
_____ 5 cooperation with municipalities
_____ 6 cooperation with non-governmental organizations
_____ 7 sponsor search
_____ 8 assistance from sponsors
_____ 9 other solutions: ______________________
_____ 10 there was no need for these kinds of solutions

4) Since the establishment of the CFAC, which of the following people has had direct telephone contact or a meeting with the voivod with regard to the lack of resources in your CFAC?				**Did the intervention bring a positive result for the CFAC?**		
	No	Yes	I don't know	**No**	**Yes**	**I don't know**
4.1 your county president	0	1	2	**0**	**1**	**2**
4.2 director of the County Family Assistance Center	0	1	2	**0**	**1**	**2**
4.3 other person: ______________________	0	1	2	**0**	**1**	**2**

5) In your opinion, the following has the greatest influence on the financing of *county tasks* in the area of social welfare in your county: (please choose only one answer)

_____ 1 parliament
_____ 2 Ministry of Finance
_____ 3 Ministry of Labor and Social Policy
_____ 4 voivodship governor [appointed by the central government]
_____ 5 county council
_____ 6 county president
_____ 7 County Family Assistance Center
_____ 8 other institution, organization, or person: ______________________

6) Were you hired for your position based on considerations that were . . .
(please choose one answer)

_____ 1 merit-based
_____ 2 political
_____ 3 merit-based and political
_____ 4 difficult to say

7) The County Strategy for Solving Social Problems is used:
(please mark all appropriate answers)

_____ 1 by municipalities in the county
_____ 2 during sessions of the county council
_____ 3 by the county administration
_____ 4 by the county president
_____ 5 in the CFAC in planning future activities in the county
_____ 6 in the Social Affairs Department in the voivodship administration (or its counterpart)
_____ 7 in the Regional Social Policy Center (or its counterpart) in the voivodship self-government
_____ 8 other possibilities: ______________________
_____ 9 there is a strategy but it is not used
_____ 10 there is no developed strategy

8) What kind of participation do the named institutions have in the development of the County Strategy for Solving Social Problems?	None	Identification of social needs	Identification of social resources	Establishment of goals of the Strategy	There are no such institutions in the county
8.1 Municipal Social Assistance Centers	0	1	2	3	
8.2 Social Assistance Homes	0	1	2	3	9
8.3 Secular and religious NGOs	0	1	2	3	9
8.4 Private companies	0	1	2	3	9
8.5 Health care facilities	0	1	2	3	9
8.6 County Labor Office	0	1	2	3	
8.7 County administration	0	1	2	3	
8.8 Schools	0	1	2	3	
8.9 Churches/parishes	0	1	2	3	
8.10 Municipal administrations	0	1	2	3	
8.11 Other ______________________		1	2	3	

9) Generally, after the 1999 administrative reform the *distance* (in kilometers) to the place of the following services for recipients is:		Less	The same	Greater
9.1	referrals to social assistance homes	0	1	2
9.2	foster families	0	1	2
9.3	services for the disabled	0	1	2

10) Generally, after the 1999 administrative reform *accessibility* to the following services for people in this county is:		Much worse	Worse	The same	Better	Much better	I don't know
10.1	social assistance homes	0	1	2	3	4	5
10.2	support centers for the mentally ill	0	1	2	3	4	5
10.3	juvenile delinquent centers	0	1	2	3	4	5

11) What political option dominates . . .		Left	Left-center coalition	Center	Right-center coalition	Right	Lack of a clear domination	I don't know
11.1	in the county council?	0	1	2	3	4	8	9
11.2	in the voivodship parliament?	0	1	2	3	4	8	9

	Weak	Average	Strong	I don't know
12) The influence of the political opposition in the county is . . .	0	1	2	3

13) Since the establishment of the CFAC, how often have you had the following forms of contact with the Social Affairs Department (or its counterpart) in the voivodship administration?		Write the approximate number of times:	**Did these contacts bring positive results?**				
			Decidedly not	**Rather not**	**Neither yes nor no**	**Rather yes**	**Decidedly yes**
13.1	Telephone contact to discuss insufficient resources		**0**	**1**	**2**	**3**	**4**
13.2	Telephone consultation of incoherent regulations		**0**	**1**	**2**	**3**	**4**
13.3	Meetings to discuss insufficient resources		**0**	**1**	**2**	**3**	**4**
13.4	Meetings, consultation of incoherent regulations		**0**	**1**	**2**	**3**	**4**
13.5	Letters or faxes regarding insufficienct resources		**0**	**1**	**2**	**3**	**4**
13.6	Letters or faxes consulting incoherent regulations		**0**	**1**	**2**	**3**	**4**
13.7	Reports on completed tasks and needs		**0**	**1**	**2**	**3**	**4**
13.8	Trainings and conferences		**0**	**1**	**2**	**3**	**4**
13.9	Other meeting(s)		**0**	**1**	**2**	**3**	**4**

14) Since the establishment of the CFAC, how often have you had the following forms of contact with the Regional Social Policy Center (or its counterpart) in the voivodship self-government?		Write the approximate number of times:	**Did these contacts bring positive results?**				
			Decidedly not	**Rather not**	**Neither yes nor no**	**Rather yes**	**Decidedly yes**
14.1	Telephone contact to discuss insufficient resources		**0**	**1**	**2**	**3**	**4**
14.2	Telephone consultation of incoherent regulations		**0**	**1**	**2**	**3**	**4**

14) Since the establishment of the CFAC, how often have you had the following forms of contact with the Regional Social Policy Center (or its counterpart) in the voivodship self-government?	Write the approximate number of times:	**Did these contacts bring positive results?**				
		Decidedly not	**Rather not**	**Neither yes nor no**	**Rather yes**	**Decidedly yes**
14.3 Meetings to discuss insufficient resources		**0**	**1**	**2**	**3**	**4**
14.4 Meetings, consultation of incoherent regulations		**0**	**1**	**2**	**3**	**4**
14.5 Letters or faxes regarding insufficient resources		**0**	**1**	**2**	**3**	**4**
14.6 Letters or faxes consulting incoherent regulations		**0**	**1**	**2**	**3**	**4**
14.7 Reports on completed tasks and needs		**0**	**1**	**2**	**3**	**4**
14.8 Trainings and conferences		**0**	**1**	**2**	**3**	**4**
14.9 Other meeting(s)		**0**	**1**	**2**	**3**	**4**

15) Please define to what degree you know the director of…	I don't know	I know by sight	I've spoken with him/her a couple of times	I've spoken with him/her many times	He/she is my acquaintance	He/she is my friend
15.1 the Social Affairs Department (or its counterpart) in the voivodship administration?	0	1	2	3	4	5
15.2 Regional Social Policy Center (or its counterpart) in the voivodship self-government?	0	1	2	3	4	5

16) Does your county have its seat in a city with county status? If yes, please answer the following questions:	Definitely no	Rather no	Rather yes	Definitely yes	I don't have an opinion
16.1 Is cooperation between the CFAC and the city CFAC going well?	0	1	2	3	4
16.2 Is there duplication of "county" social services in the city?	0	1	2	3	4
16.3 Is there rivalry between the CFAC and the city CFAC?	0	1	2	3	4
16.4 Are inhabitants from your county and from the city able to easily find the right social service institutions for them?		1	2	3	4

17) Please mark those tasks which are realized in cooperation with secular and religious non-governmental organizations:	Commission in the form of a written contract	Subsidy	Other informal cooperation
17.1 Organizing and assuring services in social assistance homes.	1	2	3
17.2 Referral of people to social assistance homes.	1	2	3
17.3 Provision of information regarding laws and rights.	1	2	3
17.4 Organizing specialized counseling.	1	2	3
17.5 Development of a county strategy for solving social problems.	1	2	3
17.6 Management of a crisis intervention center.	1	2	3
17.7 Assuring the training and professional improvement of social service staff.	1	2	3
17.8 Counseling in methods for Municipal Social Assistance Centers.	1	2	3

17) Please mark those tasks which are realized in cooperation with secular and religious non-governmental organizations:	Commission in the form of a written contract	Subsidy	Other informal cooperation
17.9 Financing county support centers (except those for the mentally ill).	1	2	3
17.10 Assistance in integration for people leaving various kinds of juvenile delinquent centers, institutions for minors, and foster families.	1	2	3
17.11 Organization and management of juvenile delinquent centers.	1	2	3
17.12 Organizing and assuring county support centers for the mentally ill.	1	2	3
17.13 Provision of monetary assistance for people leaving various kinds of juvenile delinquent centers, institutions for minors, and foster families.	1	2	3
17.14 Organizing care in foster families.	1	2	3
17.15 Provision of monetary assistance to partly cover the costs of children in foster families.	1	2	3
17.16 Assistance for refugees.	1	2	3
17.17 Assuring resources for payment of workers realizing tasks from the central government administration in the county.	1	2	3
17.18 Realization of tasks of the National Fund for Rehabilitation of the Disabled (NFRD).	1	2	3

18) What kinds of other roles do non-governmental organizations (religious and secular) have in the context of cooperation with your CFAC? (please mark all appropriate answers)

_____ 1 They realize other tasks than those named above with the support of the CFAC.
_____ 2 They play the role of advocate for local community needs and are a pressure group on the county council in matters of local needs including those of CFAC clients.
_____ 3 They participate in deciding on the division of resources from national funds (i.e. NFRD)
_____ 4 They provide the CFAC with appropriate information on a chosen social problem.
_____ 5 Other role: _____

19) Does your county co-finance some kinds of social assistance services with other counties?

_____ yes _____ no (please go to question 23)

20) Which services are co-financed?
(please mark all appropriate answers)

_____ 1 eligibility determination for the disabled
_____ 2 organizing care in foster families
_____ 3 juvenile delinquent centers
_____ 4 organizing specialized counseling
_____ 5 operating crisis intervention centers
_____ 6 support centers for the mentally ill
_____ 7 other support centers
_____ 8 other services: _____

21) The county co-finances service with other counties for what reason?
(please mark all appropriate answers)

_____ 1 the number of people needing these services is too small in each county
_____ 2 the amount of resources assigned to these services is too small
_____ 3 people are used to this place of service provision
_____ 4 lack of appropriate infrastructure in one of the cooperating counties
_____ 5 lack of people with appropriate education in one of the cooperating counties
_____ 6 other reason: _____

22) What is the overall effect of this cooperation?
(please mark all appropriate answers)

_____ 1 good, because otherwise these services would not be realized at all
_____ 2 good, because the county saves money
_____ 3 good, because the quality of the service is better
_____ 4 bad, because one of the cooperating counties is not keeping the agreement
_____ 5 bad, because the quality of the service is poor
_____ 6 bad, because the distance to the place of service for some recipients is great
_____ 7 other effect: _____

23) If you would like to better explain your above answers—please do so here.
(please write the number of the question)

24) What do you consider the greatest success of your CFAC?

Personal Demographics.

25) Gender:
______ 1) Female
______ 2) Male

26) Age:
______ 1) 25–30 years
______ 2) 31–40
______ 3) 41–50
______ 4) 51–60
______ 5) above 60 years

27) Education:
______ 1) secondary
______ 2) incomplete higher
______ 3) higher, in a higher vocational school with a specialty in "social work"
______ 4) higher, policy and social sciences
______ 5) higher, education
______ 6) higher, psychology
______ 7) higher, sociology
______ 8) higher, medicine
______ 9) higher, law
______ 10) higher, engineering
______ 11) higher, agriculture
______ 12) other: ______________________________

28) Do you have a specialization in the area of social welfare?
______ 1) Yes
______ 2) No
______ 3) I am in the process of doing a specialization

29) Previous place of work: ______________________________

30) Position in your previous place of work: ______________________________

31) Which political group do you sympathize with?

____
(name of party)

Original County Survey in Polish

ANKIETA
Do Dyrektorów/Kierowników Powiatowych
Centrów Pomocy Rodzinie

POWIAT

Powiat ______________________________ Województwo __________
Ankieter______________________________ Data ________________
Data Powstania PCPR-u ____________________________________

Niniejsze badania są rezultatem współpracy zespołu badawczego Centrum Samorządu Terytorialnego i Rozwoju Lokalnego Uniwersytetu Warszawskiego, Związku Powiatów Polskich, i Janelle Kerlin, doktorantki z Uniwersytetu Syracuse, USA. Badanie ma na celu poznanie stanu pomocy społecznej po reformie administracyjnej 1999r. Pracownia Badań Społecznych w Sopocie przeprowadza te badania w 99 losowo wybranych powiatach z terenu całej Polski. Jest to badanie socjologiczne, zatem uzyskane odpowiedzi będą opracowywane zgodnie z zasadą zachowania pełnej anonimowości. To oznacza, że nikt oprócz ankietera nie będzie wiedział, jakie są Pana(i) odpowiedzi. Udział w badaniach jest dobrowolny.

Dziękujemy za współpracę!
Proszę zaznaczyć odpowiedzi krzyżykiem (X).

1. A)
Proszę określić do jakiego stopnia w Pana(i) powiecie poniższe zadania są realizowane:
(proszę wybrać tylko jedną z tych odpowiedzi)

1. B)
Jeżeli zadania były nie realizowane lub częściowo realizowane, jakie były tego *główne powody?*
(proszę wybrać nie więcej niż dwie z tych odpowiedzi)

		Nie realizowane	**Częściowo realizowane**	**Realizowane**	**Nie ma klientów w tej kategorii**	**Inna jednostka realizuje zadanie**	Brak środków finansowych	Wystarczające środki, ale brak odpowiedniego lokalu	Wystarczające środki, ale brak osób z wykształceniem do zatrudnienia	Odpowiednia kadra, ale brak szkoleń—potrzeba nowych umiejętności	Częste nowelizacje przepisów	Inny główny powód nie występujący tutaj
1.1	Kierowanie osób ubiegających się o przyjęcie do domu pomocy społecznej.	**0**	**1**	**2**	**3**	**4**	0	1	2	3	4	5
1.2	Udzielanie informacji o prawach i uprawnieniach.	**0**	**1**	**2**	**3**	**4**	0	1	2	3	4	5
1.3	Organizowanie specjalistycznego poradnictwa, w tym rodzinnego.	**0**	**1**	**2**	**3**	**4**	0	1	2	3	4	5
1.4	Opracowywanie powiatowej strategii rozwiązywania problemów społecznych.	**0**	**1**	**2**	**3**	**4**	0	1	2	3	4	5
1.5	Prowadzenie ośrodka interwencji kryzysowej.	**0**	**1**	**2**	**3**	**4**	0	1	2	3	4	5
1.6	Zapewnienie szkolenia i doskonalenia zawodowego kadr pomocy społecznej.	**0**	**1**	**2**	**3**	**4**	0	1	2	3	4	5
1.7	Doradztwo metodyczne dla Ośrodków Pomocy Społecznej.	**0**	**1**	**2**	**3**	**4**	0	1	2	3	4	5
1.8	Finansowanie powiatowych ośrodków wsparcia (oprócz tych dla osób z zaburzeniami psychicznymi).	**0**	**1**	**2**	**3**	**4**	0	1	2	3	4	5
1.9	Pomoc w integracji ze środowiskiem osób opuszczających niektóre rodzaje placówek opiekuńczo-wychowawczych, zakładów dla nieletnich i rodzin zastępczych (np. mieszkania chronione).	**0**	**1**	**2**	**3**	**4**	0	1	2	3	4	5
1.10	Organizowanie i prowadzenie placówek opiekuńczo-wychowawczych.	**0**	**1**	**2**	**3**	**4**	0	1	2	3	4	5
1.11	Organizowanie i zapewnianie funkcjonowania powiatowych ośrodków wsparcia dla osób z zaburzeniami psychicznymi.	**0**	**1**	**2**	**3**	**4**	0	1	2	3	4	5
1.12	Przyznawanie świadczenia pieniężnego dla osób opuszczających niektóre rodzaje placówek opiekuńczo-wychowawczych, zakładów dla nieletnich i rodzin zastępczych.	**0**	**1**	**2**	**3**	**4**	0	1	2	3	4	5
1.13	Organizowanie opieki w rodzinach zastępczych.	**0**	**1**	**2**	**3**	**4**	0	1	2	3	4	5
1.14	Udzielanie pomocy pieniężnej na częściowe pokrycie kosztów utrzymania dzieci w rodzinach zastępczych.	**0**	**1**	**2**	**3**	**4**	0	1	2	3	4	5
1.15	Pomoc uchodźcom.	**0**	**1**	**2**	**3**	**4**	0	1	2	3	4	5
1.16	Zapewnianie środków na wynagrodzenia pracowników powiatu realizujących zadania z zakresu administracji rządowej.	**0**	**1**	**2**	**3**	**4**	0	1	2	3	4	5
1.17	Realizacja zadań Państwowego Funduszu Rehabilitacji Osób Niepełnosprawnych (PFRON).	**0**	**1**	**2**	**3**	**4**	0	1	2	3	4	5

2) Według Pana(i) w jakim stopniu rządowe i samorządowe środki finansowe pokrywały potrzeby w zakresie następujących zadań?* * bez transferów z innych jednostek samorządowych niż własny powiat		**1999r.**					1 styczeń 2000–15 czerwiec 2000				
		0%	**25%**	**50%**	**75%**	**100%**	0%	25%	50%	75%	100%
2.1	Organizowanie specjalistycznego poradnictwa, w tym rodzinnego.	**0**	**1**	**2**	**3**	**4**	0	1	2	3	4
2.2	Zapewnianie usług w domu pomocy społecznej (jeśli są DPS w powiecie).	**0**	**1**	**2**	**3**	**4**	0	1	2	3	4
2.3	Opracowywanie powiatowej strategii rozwiązywania problemów społecznych.	**0**	**1**	**2**	**3**	**4**	0	1	2	3	4
2.4	Prowadzenie ośrodka interwencji kryzysowej.	**0**	**1**	**2**	**3**	**4**	0	1	2	3	4
2.5	Zapewnienie szkolenia i doskonalenia zawodowego kadr pomocy społecznej.	**0**	**1**	**2**	**3**	**4**	0	1	2	3	4
2.6	Doradztwo metodyczne dla Ośrodków Pomocy Społecznej.	**0**	**1**	**2**	**3**	**4**	0	1	2	3	4
2.7	Finansowanie powiatowych ośrodków wsparcia (oprócz tych dla osób z zaburzeniami psychicznymi).	**0**	**1**	**2**	**3**	**4**	0	1	2	3	4
2.8	Pomoc w integracji ze środowiskiem osób opuszczających niektóre rodzaje placówek opiekuńczo-wychowawczych, zakładów dla nieletnich i rodzin zastępczych.	**0**	**1**	**2**	**3**	**4**	0	1	2	3	4
2.9	Organizowanie i prowadzenie placówek opiekuńczo-wychowawczych.	**0**	**1**	**2**	**3**	**4**	0	1	2	3	4
2.10	Organizowanie i zapewnianie funkcjonowania powiatowych ośrodków wsparcia dla osób z zaburzeniami psychicznymi.	**0**	**1**	**2**	**3**	**4**	0	1	2	3	4
2.11	Przyznawanie świadczenia pieniężnego dla osób opuszczających niektóre rodzaje placówek opiekuńczo-wychowawczych, zakładów dla nieletnich i rodzin zastępczych.	**0**	**1**	**2**	**3**	**4**	0	1	2	3	4
2.12	Udzielanie pomocy pieniężnej na częściowe pokrycie kosztów utrzymania dzieci w rodzinach zastępczych.	**0**	**1**	**2**	**3**	**4**	0	1	2	3	4
2.13	Pomoc uchodźcom.	**0**	**1**	**2**	**3**	**4**	0	1	2	3	4
2.14	Zapewnianie środków na wynagrodzenia pracowników powiatu realizujących zadania z zakresu administracji rządowej.	**0**	**1**	**2**	**3**	**4**	0	1	2	3	4
2.15	Realizacja zadań Państwowego Funduszu Rehabilitacji Osób Niepełnosprawnych (PFRON).	**0**	**1**	**2**	**3**	**4**	0	1	2	3	4

3) Czy w przypadku braku środków finansowych Pana(i) PCPR skorzystał z następujących rozwiązań?
(proszę zaznaczyć wszystkie właściwe odpowiedzi)

_____ 1 uruchomienie rezerw wojewody
_____ 2 uruchomienie rezerw powiatowych
_____ 3 wygospodarowanie środków z funduszy przeznaczonych na zadanie zlecone powiatowi
_____ 4 współpraca z innymi powiatami
_____ 5 współpraca z gminami
_____ 6 współpraca z organizacjami pozarządowymi
_____ 7 szukanie sponsorów
_____ 8 pomoc sponsorów
_____ 9 inne rozwiązania: ________________________________
_____ 10 nie było potrzeby takich rozwiązań

4) Czy od założenia PCPR-u niektóre z następujących osób miały bezpośredni kontakt telefoniczny czy spotkanie z *wojewodą* w sprawie niedoboru środków w Pana(i) PCPR?				**Czy interwencja przyniosła pozytywny skutek dla PCPR?**		
	Nie	Tak	Nie wiem	**Nie**	**Tak**	**Nie wiem**
4.1 starosta pana(i) powiatu	0	1	2	**0**	**1**	**2**
4.2 dyrektor Powiatowego Centrum Pomocy Rodzinie	0	1	2	**0**	**1**	**2**
4.3 inna osoba ___________________________	0	1	2	**0**	**1**	**2**

5) Pana(i) zdaniem, największy wpływ na finansowanie *zadań własnych* z zakresu pomocy społecznej w Pana(i) powiecie ma:
(proszę wybrać tylko jedną odpowiedź)
_____ 1 Sejm
_____ 2 Ministerstwo Finansów
_____ 3 Ministerstwo Pracy i Polityki Społecznej
_____ 4 Wojewoda
_____ 5 Rada Powiatu
_____ 6 Starosta
_____ 7 PCPR
_____ 8 inna instytucja, organizacja, lub osoba: ___________________________

6) Czy Pan(i) został(a) powołany(a) na stanowisko raczej z uwagi na względy . . .
(proszę wybrać jedną odpowiedź)
_____ 1 merytoryczne
_____ 2 polityczne
_____ 3 merytoryczne i polityczne
_____ 4 trudno powiedzieć

7) Powiatowa Strategia Rozwiązywania Problemów Społecznych jest wykorzystywana:
(proszę zaznaczyć wszystkie właściwe odpowiedzi)
_____ 1 przez gminy w powiecie
_____ 2 na posiedzeniu Rady Powiatu
_____ 3 przez Starostwo
_____ 4 przez Starostę
_____ 5 w PCPR przy planowaniu przyszłych działań na terenie powiatu
_____ 6 w Wydziale Spraw Społecznych (albo odpowiednik) w Urzędzie Wojewódzkim
_____ 7 w Regionalnym Ośrodku Polityki Społecznej (albo odpowiednik) w samorządzie wojewódzkim
_____ 8 inne możliwości: ___________________________
_____ 9 strategia jest, ale nie jest wykorzystywana
_____ 10 nie ma opracowanej strategii

8) Jaki jest udział wymienionych instytucji w opracowaniu Powiatowej Strategii Rozwiązywania Problemów Społecznych?	Żaden	Identyfikacja potrzeb socjalnych	Identyfikacja zasobów socjalnych	Ustalenie celów Strategii	Nie ma takich instytucji w powiecie
8.1 Ośrodki Pomocy Społecznej	0	1	2	3	
8.2 Domy Pomocy Społecznej	0	1	2	3	9
8.3 Świeckie i wyznaniowe organizacje Pozarządowe	0	1	2	3	9
8.4 Prywatne firmy	0	1	2	3	9
8.5 Zakłady Opieki Zdrowotnej	0	1	2	3	9
8.6 Urząd Pracy	0	1	2	3	
8.7 Starostwo	0	1	2	3	
8.8 Szkoły	0	1	2	3	
8.9 Kościoły/parafie	0	1	2	3	
8.10 Urzędy gminy	0	1	2	3	
8.11 Inna ___________________		1	2	3	

9) Generalnie, po reformie administracyjnej 1999r. *odległość* (w kilometrach) do miejsca poniższych usług dla odbiorców jest:		Mniejsza	Taka sama	Większa
9.1	wydawanie skierowań do Domu Pomocy Społecznej	0	1	2
9.2	usługi dla rodzin zastępczych	0	1	2
9.3	usługi dla niepełnosprawnych	0	1	2

10) Generalnie, po reformie administracyjnej 1999r. *dostępność* poniższych usług dla ludzi w tym powiecie jest:		Dużo gorsza	Gorsza	Taka sama	Lepsza	Dużo lepsza	Nie wiem
10.1	Domy Pomocy Społecznej	0	1	2	3	4	5
10.2	ośrodki wsparcia dla osób z zaburzeniami psychicznymi	0	1	2	3	4	5
10.3	placówki opiekuńczo-wychowawcze	0	1	2	3	4	5

11) Jaka opcja polityczna dominuje . . .		Lewicowa	Koalicja Lewicowo-centrowa	Centrum	Koalicja Prawicowo-centrowa	Prawicowa	Brak wyraźnej dominacji	Nie wiem
11.1	w radzie powiatu?	0	1	2	3	4	8	9
11.2	w wojewódzkim sejmiku?	0	1	2	3	4	8	9

	Słaby	Średni	Silny	Nie Wiem
12) Wpływ opozycji partyjnej w powiecie jest:	0	1	2	3

13) Od założenia PCPR jak często Pan(i) miał(a) następujące formy kontaktu z Wydziałem Spraw Społecznych Urzędu Wojewódzkiego (albo odpowiednik)?		Napisz w przybliżeniu ile razy:	Czy te kontakty przyniosły pozytywne skutki?				
			Zdecydowanie nie	**Raczej nie**	**Ani tak, ani nie**	**Raczej tak**	**Zdecydowanie tak**
13.1	Kontakt telefoniczny w sprawie niedoboru środków		**0**	**1**	**2**	**3**	**4**
13.2	Konsultacje telefoniczne nt. Niespójności przepisów		**0**	**1**	**2**	**3**	**4**
13.3	Wspólne spotkania w sprawie niedoboru środków		**0**	**1**	**2**	**3**	**4**
13.4	Wspólne spotkania, konsultacje niespójnych przepisów		**0**	**1**	**2**	**3**	**4**
13.5	Listy lub faxy w sprawie niedoboru środków		**0**	**1**	**2**	**3**	**4**
13.6	Listy lub faxy konsultujące niespójne przepisy		**0**	**1**	**2**	**3**	**4**
13.7	Sprawozdania z realizowanych zadań i potrzeb		**0**	**1**	**2**	**3**	**4**
13.8	Szkolenia i narady		**0**	**1**	**2**	**3**	**4**
13.9	Inne spotkanie(a)		**0**	**1**	**2**	**3**	**4**

14) Od założenia PCPR jak często Pan(i) miał(a) następujące formy kontaktu z Regionalnym Ośrodkiem Polityki Społecznej (albo odpowiednik) w samorządzie wojewódzkim?	Napisz w przybliżeniu ile razy:	Czy te kontakty przyniosły pozytywne skutki? Zdecydowanie nie	Raczej nie	Ani tak, ani nie	Raczej tak	Zdecydowanie tak
14.1 Kontakt telefoniczny w sprawie niedoboru środków		0	1	2	3	4
14.2 Konsultacje telefoniczne nt. Niespójności przepisów		0	1	2	3	4
14.3 Wspólne spotkania w sprawie niedoboru środków		0	1	2	3	4
14.4 Wspólne spotkania, konsultacje niespójnych przepisów		0	1	2	3	4
14.5 Listy lub faxy w sprawie niedoboru środków		0	1	2	3	4
14.6 Listy lub faxy konsultujące niespójne przepisy		0	1	2	3	4
14.7 Sprawozdania z realizowanych zadań i potrzeb		0	1	2	3	4
14.8 Szkolenia i narady		0	1	2	3	4
14.9 Inne spotkanie(a)		0	1	2	3	4

15) Proszę określić w jakim stopniu zna Pan(i) dyrektora . . .	Nie znam	Znam z widzenia	Kilka razy z nim/nią rozmawiałam	Wiele razy z nim/nią rozmawiałam	Jest moją znajomą	Jest moim kolegą/moją koleżanką
15.1 Wydziału Spraw Społecznych Urzędu Wojewódzkiego (albo odpowiednik)?	0	1	2	3	4	5
15.2 Regionalnego Ośrodka Polityki Społecznej (albo odpowiednik) w samorządzie wojewódzkim?	0	1	2	3	4	5

16) Jeśli Pana(i) powiat ma siedzibę w mieście na prawach powiatu proszę odpowiedzieć na następujące pytania:	Zdecydowanie nie	Raczej nie	Raczej tak	Zdecydowanie tak	Nie mam zdania
16.1 Czy współpraca PCPR z MOPS/MOPR-em układa się dobrze?	0	1	2	3	4
16.2 Czy „powiatowe" usługi socjalne dublują się na terenie miasta?	0	1	2	3	4
16.3 Czy jest rywalizacja między PCPR-em a MOPS/MOPR-em?	0	1	2	3	4
16.4 Czy mieszkańcy z Pana(i) powiatu i z miasta na prawach powiatu łatwo trafiają do właściwych dla nich instytucji pomocy społecznej?	0	1	2	3	4

17) Proszę zaznaczyć te zadania, które są realizowane we współpracy z świeckimi lub wyznaniowymi organizacjami pozarządowymi:	Zlecenie w formie pisemnego kontraktu	Dotacja	Inna współpraca nieformalna
17.1 Organizowanie i zapewnianie usług w domu pomocy społecznej. Kierowanie osób ubiegających się o przyjęcie do domu pomocy społecznej.	1	2	3
17.3 Udzielanie informacji o prawach i uprawnieniach.	1	2	3
17.4 Organizowanie specjalistycznego poradnictwa.	1	2	3
17.5 Opracowywanie powiatowej strategii rozwiązywania problemów społecznych.	1	2	3
17.6 Prowadzenie ośrodka interwencji kryzysowej.	1	2	3
17.7 Zapewnienie szkolenia i doskonalenia zawodowego kadr pomocy społecznej.	1	2	3
17.8 Doradztwo metodyczne dla Ośrodków Pomocy Społecznej.	1	2	3
17.9 Finansowanie powiatowych ośrodków wsparcia (oprócz tych dla osób z zaburzeniami psychicznymi).	1	2	3
17.10 Pomoc w integracji ze środowiskiem osób opuszczających niektóre rodzaje placówek opiekuńczo-wychowawczych, zakładów dla nieletnich i rodzin zastępczych.	1	2	3
17.11 Organizowanie i prowadzenie placówek opiekuńczo-wychowawczych.	1	2	3
17.12 Organizowanie i zapewnianie funkcjonowania powiatowych ośrodków wsparcia dla osób z zaburzeniami psychicznymi.	1	2	3
17.13 Przyznawanie świadczenia pieniężnego dla osób opuszczających niektóre rodzaje placówek opiekuńczo-wychowawczych, zakładów dla nieletnich i rodzin zastępczych.	1	2	3
17.14 Organizowanie opieki w rodzinach zastępczych.	1	2	3
17.15 Udzielanie pomocy pieniężnej na częściowe pokrycie kosztów dzieci w rodzinach zastępczych.	1	2	3
17.16 Pomoc uchodźcom.	1	2	3
17.17 Zapewnianie środków na wynagrodzenia pracowników realizujących zadania z zakresu administracji rządowej realizowanych przez powiat.	1	2	3
17.18 Realizacja zadań Państwowego Funduszu Rehabilitacji Osób Niepełnosprawnych (PFRON).	1	2	3

18) Jakie są inne role organizacji pozarządowych (świeckich i wyznaniowych) w ramach współpracy z Pana(i) PCPR-em? (proszę zaznaczyć wszystkie właściwe odpowiedzi)

_____ 1 Realizują inne zadania niż wyżej wymienione przy wsparciu PCPR-u.
_____ 2 Odgrywają rolę rzecznika potrzeb lokalnych społeczności i są grupę nacisku na radę powiatu w sprawach potrzeb wspólnot lokalnych w tym klientów PCPR-u.
_____ 3 Mają udział w opiniowaniu przydzielania środków z funduszy publicznych na poziomie powiatowym (np. PFRON).
_____ 4 Zapewniają PCPR odpowiednie informacje nt. wybranego problem społecznego.
_____ 5 Inna rola: ______________________________

19) Czy Pan(i) powiat współfinansuje niektóre usługi pomocy społecznej z innymi powiatami?

_____ tak _____ nie (proszę przejść do pytania 23)

20) Jakie usługi są współfinansowane?
(proszę zaznaczyć wszystkie właściwe odpowiedzi)

_____ 1 orzekanie o stopniu niepełnosprawności
_____ 2 organizowanie opieki w rodzinach zastępczych
_____ 3 placówki opiekuńczo-wychowawcze
_____ 4 organizowanie specjalistycznego poradnictwa
_____ 5 prowadzenie ośrodka interwencji kryzysowej
_____ 6 ośrodki wsparcia dla osób z zaburzeniami psychicznymi
_____ 7 pozostałe ośrodki wsparcia
_____ 8 inne usługi: ______________________________

21) Z jakiego powodu powiat współfinansuje usługi z innymi powiatami?
(proszę zaznaczyć wszystkie właściwe odpowiedzi)
_____ 1 zbyt mała liczba osób potrzebujących tych usług w jednym powiecie
_____ 2 zbyt małe środki przeznaczone na takie usługi
_____ 3 ludzie są przyzwyczajeni do tego miejsca dostarczania świadczeń
_____ 4 brak odpowiedniej infrastruktury w jednym z współpracujących powiatów
_____ 5 brak osób z odpowiednim wykształceniem w jednym z współpracujących powiatów
_____ 6 inny powód: ____________________

22) Jaki jest ogólny efekt tej współpracy?
(proszę zaznaczyć wszystkie właściwe odpowiedzi)
_____ 1 dobry, bo inaczej takie usługi nie byłyby realizowane w ogóle
_____ 2 dobry, bo powiaty oszczędzają pieniądze
_____ 3 dobry, bo jest lepsza jakość usług
_____ 4 zły, bo jeden z współpracujących powiatów nie wywiązuje się z umowy
_____ 5 zły, bo jakość usług nie jest dobra
_____ 6 zły, bo odległość do miejsca usług dla niektórych odbiorców jest duża
_____ 7 inny efekt: ____________________

23) Jeśli Pan(i) chciał(a)by szerszej skomentować powyższe odpowiedzi-proszę o uwagi:
(proszę napisać numer pytania)

24) Co uważa Pan(i) za największy sukces PCPR-u?

Metryczka.

25) Płeć:
_____ 1) kobieta
_____ 2) mężczyzna

26) Wiek:
_____ 1) 25–30 lat
_____ 2) 31–40
_____ 3) 41–50
_____ 4) 51–60
_____ 5) powyżej 60 lat.

27) Wykształcenie:
_____ 1) średnie
_____ 2) niepełne wyższe
_____ 3) wyższe w wyższej szkole zawodowej o specjalności „praca socjalna"
_____ 4) wyższe, politologia i nauki społeczne
_____ 5) wyższe pedagogiczne
_____ 6) wyższe psychologiczne
_____ 7) wyższe socjologiczne
_____ 8) wyższe medyczne
_____ 9) wyższe prawnicze
_____ 10) wyższe techniczne
_____ 11) wyższe rolnicze
_____ 12) inne: ____________________

28) Specjalizacja w zakresie pomocy społecznej?
_____ 1) Tak
_____ 2) Nie
_____ 3) Jestem w trakcie robienia specjalizacji

29) Poprzednie miejsce pracy: ____________________

30) Stanowisko w poprzednim miejscu pracy: ____________________

31) Z jakim ugrupowaniem politycznym Pan(i) sympatyzuje?
____
(nazwa partii, stronnictwa)

Notes

Chapter 1

1. For a discussion on the utility of disjointed pluralism versus collective interest see Eric Schickler, *Disjointed Pluralism: Institutional Innovation and the Development of the U.S. Congress.*
2. Ibid., p. 4 (emphasis in the original).
3. Ibid., p. 3.
4. Haggard and Webb demonstrate that processes and behaviors similar to those Schickler bases his ideas on are at work in postcommunist democratic settings. Their definition of policy in this context as "the outcome of interactions among politicians, bureaucrats, and interest groups operating within a set of institutional constraints" illustrates this point. See Stephan Haggard and S. B. Webb, "Introduction," in *Voting for Reform: Democracy, Political Liberalization, and Economic Adjustment,* p. 3
5. For a discussion on the approach of neoliberals to reform development in transitioning countries see Béla Greskovits, *The Political Economy of Protest and Patience.*
6. Though providing a less-than-favorable critique of the democratic politics of reform in terms of meeting reform goals, this study is not intended as a negative critique of democracy as a form of government. A critique of democracy necessarily involves the weighing in of other values that are generally considered more important than immediate attainment of any one party's reform goals. Indeed, democracy is most valued because of its ability to peacefully mediate between and reflect different interests and opinions, which is precisely what this study shows is happening in Poland.
7. Jerzy Regulski, *Samorząd III Rzeczypospolitej—Koncepcje i Realizacja;* R. Bird, R. Ebel, and C. Wallich, "Fiscal Decentralization: From Command to Market," in *Decentralization of the Socialist State;* Joanna Regulska, "Local Government Reform," in *Transition to Democracy in Poland,* ed. Richard Staar; J. Zaucha, "Regional and Local Development in Poland," in *Decentralization and Transition in the Visegrad,* ed. E. Kirchner; Jolanta Koral, "Sukcesy i Porażki Wdrażanej Reformy" in *Cztery Reformy: Od Koncepcji do Realizacji,* ed. L. Kolarska-Bobinska.
8. The English words "county" and "province" are used here as only approximate translations of the Polish words *"powiat"* and *"województwa"* and are not meant to connote county or province in the American or Canadian sense.
9. Regulski, *Samorząd III Rzeczypospolitej.*
10. Territorial offices in these regions were strictly organs of the state administration. They oversaw services that had been left under central government auspices with the municipal reforms because they were deemed too large for municipalities to administer. See Regulski, *Samorząd III Rzeczypospolitej.* Such services included secondary schools, health care, law enforcement, fire protection, sanitation, veterinary control, and building inspection. See Andrzej Kowalczyk, "Local Government in Poland," in *Decentralization: Experiments and Reforms,* ed. T. Horvath.
11. Special field administrations, while instituted under the Communist regime, increased in number after the municipal reforms in an effort to improve the effectiveness of central ministries. Reformers viewed this system as a "federation of ministries" because each area of state activity in a given region was managed separately, which led to conflicting and overlapping powers and policies. A number of special administrations had already been placed under provincial authority in 1996. See Józef Płoskonka, *Reforma Admin-*

istracji Publicznej, 1998–2001; B. Nunberg and L. Barbone, "Breaking Administrative Deadlock in Poland: Internal Obstacles and External Incentives," in *The State after Communism: Administrative Transitions in Central and Eastern Europe*, ed. B. Nunberg.

12. Zaucha, "Regional and Local Development in Poland"; Regulski, *Samorząd III Rzeczypospolitej.*

13. Jerzy Regulski, "Nowy Ustrój, Nowe Szanse, Nowe Problemy," in *Podstawowe Wartości i Założenia Reformy Ustrojowej—Ustrój Samorządu Terytorialnego w Polsce*; Włodzimierz Puzyna, interview with author, Warsaw, July 6, 2000; P. Fenrych and W. Puzyna, "Wielka Decentralizacja," *Więż* 6, no. 512 (2001): 14–28; Zyta Gilowska, "Reforma Samorządów a Reforma Finansów Publicznych," in *Cztery Reformy*, ed. L. Kolarska-Bobinska.

14. Cited in Ewa Leś, "Zasada Subsydiarność i jej Użyteczność w Reformowaniu Instytucji Pomocy Społecznej w Polsce," p. 2, author's translation.

15. Regulski, *Samorząd III Rzeczypospolitej*, p. 367, author's translation.

16. Ibid.; Hubert Izdebski, *Samorząd Terytorialny: Podstawy Ustroju i Działalności.*

17. Jadwiga Emilewicz and Artur Wołek, *Reformatorzy i Politycy.*

18. Mirosław Sekuła, interview with author, Warsaw, July 12, 2000.

19. Mitchell Orenstein, *Out of the Red: Building Capitalism and Democracy in Postcommunist Europe.*

20. Ibid.; S. Johnson and M. Kowalska, "Poland: The Political Economy of Shock Therapy," in *Voting for Reform*, ed. S. Haggard and S. B. Webb.

21. Michał Kulesza, *Sprawozdanie z Działalnośći Pełnomocnika Rządu ds. Reform Ustrojowych Państwa.* Though much work remained to be done, significant groundwork had been laid for the 1999 reform in the 1992–93 period (see discussion in chapter 2).

22. Lena Kolarska-Bobinska, "Wstęp," in *Cztery Reformy*; Emilewicz and Wołek, *Reformatorzy i Politycy*; Michał Kulesza, "Methods and Techniques of Managing Decentralization Reforms in CEE Countries: The Polish Experience," in *Mastering Decentralization and Public Administration Reforms in Central and Eastern Europe*, ed. Gábor Péteri.

23. Sekuła interview.

24. Kulesza, *Sprawozdanie z Działalnośći Pełnomocnika*; Puzyna interview, July 6, 2000.

25. Tony Levitas, "The Political Economy of Fiscal Decentralization and Local Government Finance Reform in Poland."

26. Michał Kulesza, the government plenipotentiary for the reform, acknowledges that the speed of the reform undermined its quality; however, in his view, speed was the only way to get ahead of the opposition and pass the reform at all. He states that "the radical changes had to be implemented in a democratic way and that is why an emperor's power had to be replaced with high pace of work as only speed could save us. That was why my aim was to implement the reform even when quality would suffer." Kulesza, "Methods and Techniques of Managing Decentralization Reforms," p. 205.

27. Emilewicz and Wołek, *Reformatorzy i Politycy*; Puzyna interview, July 6, 2000.

28. Kowalczyk, "Local Government in Poland"; Koral, "Sukcesy i Porażki Wdrażanej Reformy."

29. Regulska, "Local Government Reform," p. 118; Katarzyna Jędrzejewska, "Samorządowcy Mają Inny Pomysł na Dochody," *Rzeczpospolita*, May 26, 2000; Maria Weber, "O Nas bez Nas," *Wspólnota* 19, no. 53 (2000): 7; Puzyna interview, July 6, 2000.

30. M. Grochowski and J. Regulska, "New Partnership and Collaboration: Local Government and its Supporting Institutions—The Case of Poland," in *Towards a New Concept of Local Self-Government?*, ed. Erik Amna and Stig Montin.

31. Kulesza, *Sprawozdanie z Działalnośći Pełnomocnika.* For a discussion of the role of western assistance on local democracy reforms in Poland through 1997 see Joanna Regulska,

"Building Local Democracy: The Role of Western Assistance in Poland," *Voluntas: International Journal of Voluntary and Nonprofit Organizations* 9, no. 1 (1998): 39–57.

32. This study is an analysis of policy and what happens when mainly poor policy is implemented. It is not an implementation study where the implementation context is examined to better understand its effect on policy outcomes. However, poor policy is sometimes identified during the implementation phase; for example, two policies may be found in conflict with one another as outcomes are observed or flaws in the written legislation uncovered. In general, this study looks at poor policy that precluded desired outcomes even before the implementation stage.

33. For examples of literature on the politics of decentralization, see E. Willis, C. Garman, and S. Haggard, "The Politics of Decentralization in Latin America," *Latin American Research Review* 34, no. 1 (1999): 7–56; P. J. Luong, "The Path Least Resisted: The Politics of Economic Decentralization in Kazakhstan"; Kent Eaton, "Fiscal Decentralization in Developing Democracies: What's at Stake for Legislators?"; Martin Brusis, "Re-creating the Regional Level in Central and Eastern Europe: An Analysis of Administrative Reforms in Six Countries, in *Central and Eastern Europe on the Way into the European Union,* ed. Erik von Breska and Martin Brusis; Michal Illner, "Territorial Decentralization—A Stumbling Block of Democratic Reforms in East-Central Europe?" *Polish Sociological Review* 1, no. 117 (1997): 23–45.

34. Levitas, "The Political Economy of Fiscal Decentralization"; Teresa Ter-Minassian, "Decentralizing Government," *Finance and Development* 34, no. 3 (1997): 36–39.

35. E. Kirchner and T. Christiansen, "The Importance of Local and Regional Reform," in *Decentralization and Transition in the Visegrad,* ed. E. Kirchner; M. Rousseau and R. Zariski, *Regionalism and Regional Devolution in Comparative Perspective;* J. Huther and A. Shah, *Applying a Simple Measure of Good Governance to the Debate on Fiscal Decentralization.*

36. Jean-Paul Faguet, *Does Decentralization Increase Responsiveness to Local Needs? Evidence from Bolivia;* Harry Blair, "Participation and Accountability at the Periphery: Democratic Local Governance in Six Countries" *World Development* 28, no. 1 (2000): 21–39; S. R. Osmani, *Participatory Governance, People's Empowerment and Poverty Reduction.*

37. Remy Prud'homme, "On the Dangers of Decentralization," *The World Bank Research Observer* 10, no. 2 (1995): 201–10; Anwar Shah, *Balance, Accountability, and Responsiveness: Lessons about Decentralization;* Joanna Regulska and Jerzy Regulski, "Local Self-Government Reform in Central and Eastern Europe," in *Democracy Building Process in Central and Eastern Europe,* ed. A. Rybczynska; James Manor, *The Political Economy of Democratic Decentralization;* United Nations, *Decentralization: Conditions for Success;* M. Giugale and S. Webb, eds., *Achievements and Challenges of Fiscal Decentralization: Lessons from Mexico.*

38. Bird, Ebel, and Wallich, "Fiscal Decentralization"; Kirchner, ed., *Decentralization and Transition in the Visegrad;* Tamas M. Horvath, ed., *Decentralization: Experiments and Reforms.*

39. The term "public administration reform" has a broader meaning in Eastern Europe than it does in the United States. In Eastern Europe it is often used additionally in reference to decentralization of the state apparatus and territorial redivision of the state.

40. Brusis, "Re-creating the Regional Level in Central and Eastern Europe"; Illner, "Territorial Decentralization." Joachim J. Hesse, "Rebuilding the State: Public Sector Reform in Central and Eastern Europe," in *Public Sector Reform: Rationale, Trends and Problems,* ed. Jan-Erik Lane. Hesse's six explanatory concepts include stages of development like transformation and modernization, cultural traditions, institutional variables, the given resource base, the degree of reform professionalization, and policy entrepreneurship or political will.

41. Hellmut Wollman, "Institution Building and Decentralization in Formerly Socialist Countries: The Cases of Poland, Hungary, and East Germany," *Environment and*

Planning C: Government and Policy 15 (1997): 464. Wollman's decision-shaping factors include institutional and cognitive legacies of the past, exogenous factors (models and experiences of Western European countries), the socioeconomic and financial context, and the power, interests, and skills of actors.

42. Levitas, "The Political Economy of Fiscal Decentralization."

43. Kirchner and Christiansen, "The Importance of Local and Regional Reform"; Rousseau and Zariski, *Regionalism and Regional Devolution in Comparative Perspective;* M. Watson, "Conclusion: A Comparative Evaluation of Planning Practice in the Liberal Democratic State," in *Planning, Politics, and Public Policy: The British, French, and Italian Experience,* ed. L. Binder et al.

44. Rousseau and Zariski, *Regionalism and Regional Devolution in Comparative Perspective;* B. Smith, *Decentralization: The Territorial Dimension of the State;* D. Kettl, *Reinventing Government? Appraising the National Performance Review;* D. Osborne and T. Gaebler, *Reinventing Government.*

45. Suzanne Mettler, *Dividing Citizens: Gender and Federalism in New Deal Public Policy.*

46. Ibid.; Rousseau and Zariski, *Regionalism and Regional Devolution in Comparative Perspective;* A. Rivlin, *Reviving the American Dream;* D. Cameron and R. Hofferbert, "The Impact of Federalism on Education Finance: A Comparative Analysis," *European Journal of Political Research* 2 (Sept., 1974): 225–58.

47. Rivlin, *Reviving the American Dream;* Bird, Ebel, and Wallich, "Fiscal Decentralization"; Paul Peterson, *The Price of Federalism.*

48. See R. Nathan and T. Gais, "Early Findings about the Newest New Federalism for Welfare," *Publius* 28, no. 3 (1998): 95–103; S. Allard, "Revisiting Shapiro: Welfare Magnets and State Residency Requirements in the 1990s," *Publius* 28, no. 3 (1998): 45–65; M. Rom, P. Peterson, and K. Scheve, "Interstate Competition and Welfare Policy," *Publius* 28, no. 3 (1998): 17–37.

49. Robert Dahl, *Dilemmas of Pluralist Democracy: Autonomy vs. Control;* Mettler, *Dividing Citizens;* Rousseau and Zariski, *Regionalism and Regional Devolution in Comparative Perspective.*

50. Rivlin, *Reviving the American Dream;* Smith, *Decentralization;* Osborne and Gaebler, *Reinventing Government;* Elinor Ostrom, "Metropolitan Reform: Propositions Derived from Two Traditions," *Social Science Quarterly* 53 (1972): 474–93; Vicent Ostrom, R. Bish, and E. Ostrom, *Local Government in the United States;* Ronald J. Oakerson, *Governing Local Public Economies.*

51. Dahl, *Dilemmas of Pluralist Democracy;* Gulick cited in Dwight Waldo, *The Administrative State: A Study of the Political Theory of American Public Administration;* Ostrom, Bish, and Ostrom, *Local Government in the United States;* Oakerson, *Governing Local Public Economies.*

52. Bird, Ebel, and Wallich, "Fiscal Decentralization"; Manor, *The Political Economy of Democratic Decentralization;* Prud'homme, "On the Dangers of Decentralization"; Ter-Minassian, "Decentralizing Government."

53. Robert Yin, *Case Study Research: Design and Methods,* p. 13.

54. Horvath, *Decentralization.*

55. Yin, *Case Study Research.*

56. Floyd Fowler, *Survey Research Methods.*

57. Funding for the surveys and interviews conducted in 2000 was provided by a Fulbright-Hays Dissertation Research Abroad Fellowship, 1999–2000. Interviews conducted in 2001 were funded by an American Council of Learned Societies East European Dissertation Fellowship.

58. See chapter 4 for a more detailed description of the survey methodology used here.

59. For example, Paul Peterson says that "redistributive policy is the job of the national government" in Peterson, *The Price of Federalism,* p. xii.

60. Ibid., p. 128.

61. It is interesting to note, however, that disparity and a decrease in funding for some services occurred with the reform even though fiscal responsibility remained centralized. Disparity occurred between urban and rural areas because of differences in subnational government structure and access to resources. Funding was inadequate at times because central government tasks were decentralized without an appropriate assignment of funds or source of funding. A discussion on this topic with regard to social services is found in chapter 5.

62. Regulski, "Nowy Ustrój, Nowe Szanse, Nowe Problemy."

Chapter 2

1. Norman Davies, *God's Playground: A History of Poland, Vol I. The Origins to 1795.*

2. Antoni Kuklinski and P. Swianiewicz, "The Polish Palatinatus: Experiences and Prospects," in *The Rise of Meso Government in Europe,* ed. L.J. Sharpe.

3. Ibid.; Izdebski, *Samorząd Terytorialny.*

4. Norman Davies, *God's Playground: A History of Poland, Vol II. 1795 to the Present.*

5. Izdebski, *Samorząd Terytorialny;* Hubert Izdebski, "Samorząd Terytorialny w II Rzeczypospolitej," in *Samorząd Terytorialny: Zagadnienia Prawne i Administracyjne,* ed. Andrzej Piekara and Zygmunt Niewiadomski.

6. Kuklinski and Swianiewicz, "The Polish Palatinatus"; Izdebski, *Samorząd Terytorialny;* Regulski, *Samorząd III Rzeczypospolitej.*

7. Izdebski, *Samorząd Terytorialny;* Regulski, *Samorząd III Rzeczypospolitej.*

8. For more on democratic centralism and local government reforms in Poland from 1950 to 1970 see Ray Taras, "Democratic Centralism and Polish Local Government Reforms," *London: Public Administration* 53 (winter, 1975): 403–26.

9. Kuklinski and Swianiewicz, "The Polish Palatinatus"; Regulski, *Samorząd III Rzeczypospolitej.*

10. Grzegorz Gorzelak, "Decentralization, Regional Development and Regional Policies," in *Poland into the New Millennium,* ed. G. Blazyca and R. Rapacki.

11. Bird, Ebel, and Wallich, "Fiscal Decentralization"; Regulska, "Local Government Reform"; J. Zaucha, "Regional and Local Development in Poland"; Koral, "Sukcesy i Porażki Wdrażanej Reformy."

12. Regulski, *Samorząd III Rzeczypospolitej.*

13. Emilewicz and Wołek, *Reformatorzy i Politycy,* p. 34.

14. Regulski, *Samorząd III Rzeczypospolitej;* Emilewicz and Wołek, *Reformatorzy i Politycy;* Kulesza, *Sprawozdanie z Działalnośći Pełnomocnika.*

15. Regulski, *Samorząd III Rzeczypospolitej.*

16. Joanna Regulska, "Decentralization or (Re)Centralization: Struggle for Political Power in Poland," *Environment and Planning C: Government and Policy* 15 (1997): 187–207.

17. Ibid.

18. For a more detailed accounting of reform preparations under the Suchocka government see Kulesza, "Methods and Techniques of Managing Decentralization Reforms."

19. Regulski, *Samorząd III Rzeczypospolitej.*

20. Ibid., pp. 129–30, author's translation.

21. Ibid.

22. Emilewicz and Wołek, *Reformatorzy i Politycy.*

23. Ministerstwo Spraw Wewnętrznych i Administracji (MSWiA; Polish Ministry of Internal Affairs and Administration), *Powiaty i Miasta na Prawach Powiatu po Roku Reformy;* Tony Levitas and Jan Herczynski, "Decentralization, Local Governments and Education

Reform in Post-Communist Poland"; W. Surazska, J. Bucek, L. Malikova, and P. Danek, "Towards Regional Government in Central Europe: Territorial Restructuring of Postcommunist Regimes," *Environment and Planning C: Government and Policy* 14 (1996): 437–62.

24. Regulski, *Samorząd III Rzeczypospolitej*; Kulesza, *Sprawozdanie z Działalnośći Pełnomocnika.*
25. Irena Lipowicz, interview with author, Vienna, Aug. 7, 2000; Krzysztof Janik, interview with author, Warsaw, July 19, 2000; G. Gorzelak and B. Jałowiecki, *Analiza Procesu Wdrażania i Skutków Reformy Terytorialnej Organizacji Kraju—Raport Końcowy*; Wollman, "Institution Building and Decentralization in Formerly Socialist Countries."
26. Kulesza, "Methods and Techniques of Managing Decentralization," p. 199.
27. Janik interview; Lipowicz interview; Regulska, "Decentralization or (Re)Centralization."
28. The Institute was established using funds from the Ford Foundation and the Stefan Batory Foundation (Soros based).
29. Józef Płoskonka, interview with author, Warsaw, Mar. 8, 2001; Gorzelak and Jałowiecki, *Analiza Procesu Wdrażania.*
30. Funds were from PHARE Omega and a municipal consortium from Holland, Denmark, Belgium, and German *Länder.*
31. Professor Piekara had a history of opposing decentralization as proposed by those connected with Solidarity. He had taken part in the Round Table discussions in 1989 as a member of the government rather than of the Solidarity opposition.
32. Andrzej Piekara, interview with author, Warsaw, Mar. 6, 2001.
33. Zaucha, "Regional and Local Development in Poland," p. 76.
34. Ibid.; Kowalczyk, "Local Government in Poland."
35. Levitas and Herczynski, "Decentralization, Local Governments."
36. Chancellory of the Sejm, *The Constitution of the Republic of Poland,* pp. 4, 8, and 65.
37. Kowalczyk, "Local Government in Poland"; Lipowicz interview; Płoskonka, *Reforma Administracji Publicznej.*
38. Sekuła interview; Emilewicz and Wołek, *Reformatorzy i Politycy*; Lipowicz interview.
39. Kulesza, *Sprawozdanie z Działalnośći Pełnomocnika*; Puzyna interview, July 6, 2000.
40. Izdebski, "Samorząd Terytorialny w II Rzeczypospolitej."
41. Zaucha, "Regional and Local Development in Poland," p. 75.
42. Brusis, "Re-creating the Regional Level in Central and Eastern Europe"; Kirchner and Christiansen, "The Importance of Local and Regional Reform."
43. Płoskonka, *Reforma Administracji Publicznej*; Koral, "Sukcesy i Porażki Wdrażanej Reformy"; Emilewicz and Wołek, *Reformatorzy i Politycy.*
44. Płoskonka, *Reforma Administracji Publicznej,* p. 222, author's translation.
45. The word 'rationalize,' used in the context of administrative reform throughout the text, means to bring modern, efficient methods to a system.
46. Chancellory of the President of the Council of Ministers, *Ogólne Założenia Reformy Ustrojowej Państwa,* p. 25, author's translation.

Chapter 3

1. World Bank, *The Online Sourcebook on Decentralization and Local Government.*
2. Haggard and Webb, "Introduction," p. 8.
3. New institutionalism is a branch of public policy analysis "concentrated on identifying key institutional features that affect the way in which actors interact in the formulation of policy, and as a result have an impact on policy outcomes," Giuliano Bonoli, *The Politics of Pension Reform: Institutions and Policy Change in Western Europe,* p. 39.

Historical institutionalism and path dependency are subsumed under new institutionalism.

4. Michael Cain and Aleksander Surdej, "Transitional Politics or Public Choice? Evaluating Stalled Pension Reforms in Poland," in *Left Parties and Social Policy in Postcommunist Europe,* ed. L. Cook, M. Orenstein, and M. Rueschemeyer.

5. Stephan Haggard and Robert Kaufman, *The Political Economy of Democratic Transitions;* Samuel Huntington, *The Third Wave: Democratisation in the Late 20th Century;* Juan J. Linz and Alfred Stepan, *Problems of Democratic Transition and Consolidation: South America and Post-Communist Europe;* S. White, J. Blatt, and P. Lewis, eds., *Developments in East European Politics;* Valerie Bunce, "The Political Economy of Postsocialism," *Slavic Review* 58, no. 4 (1999): 756–93.

6. Alberto Alesina, "Political Models of Macroeconomic Policy and Fiscal Reforms," in *Voting for Reform,* ed. S. Haggard and S. Webb; M. Kaminski, G. Lissowski, and P. Swistak, "The 'Revival of Communism' or the Effect of Institutions? The 1993 Polish Parliamentary Elections," *Public Choice* 97, no. 3 (1998): 429–50; Mancur Olson, "The Devolution of Power in Post-Communist Societies: Therapies for Corruption, Fragmentation and Economic Retardation," in *Russia's Stormy Path to Reform,* ed. R. Skidelsky; Adam Przeworksi, *Democracy and the Market.*

7. Cain and Surdej, "Transitional Politics or Public Choice?," p. 146.

8. Brusis, "Re-creating the Regional Level in Central and Eastern Europe"; Illner, "Territorial Decentralization"; Hesse, "Rebuilding the State"; Wollman, "Institution Building and Decentralization in Formerly Socialist Countries." A brief discussion of these authors' approaches can be found in chapter 1.

9. Greskovits, *The Political Economy of Protest and Patience.*

10. Schickler, *Disjointed Pluralism,* pp. 267–68.

11. Only three of Schickler's four claims about disjointed pluralism are examined here. The one missing claim is based on examination of chronological factors in Schickler's four cases, factors that are missing in the four cases presented here because they are not chronological.

12. Schickler, *Disjointed Pluralism,* p. 12.

13. Ibid., p. 13 (emphasis in the original).

14. Ibid.

15. Ibid., p. 13.

16. Ibid., p. 14.

17. Ibid., p. 15.

18. See Paul Pierson, "Increasing Returns, Path Dependence, and the Study of Politics;" Douglass North, *Institutions, Institutional Change, and Economic Performance;* Thomas F. Remington and Steven S. Smith, "Theories of Legislative Institutions and the Organization of the Russian Duma," *American Journal of Political Science* 42 (1998): 545–72.

19. Stephan Haggard and Robert Kaufman, "Introduction," in *Reforming the State: Fiscal and Welfare Reform in Post-Socialist Countries,* ed. J. Kornai, S. Haggard, and R. Kaufman, p. 16.

20. Bonoli, *The Politics of Pension Reform;* Haggard and Kaufman, "Introduction."

21. For discussions on degree of government control over parliament in parliamentary versus separation-of-powers systems see A. Lijphart, *Democracies: Pattern of Majoritarian and Consensus Government in Twenty-one Countries;* K. Weaver and B. Rockman, *Do Institutions Matter? Government Capabilities in the United States and Abroad.*

22. Bonoli, *The Politics of Pension Reform.*

23. Ibid.

24. Ibid.

25. Ibid.
26. Ibid.
27. Ibid.
28. Haggard and Webb, "Introduction," p. 9; see also N. Roubini and J. Sachs, "Political and Economic Determinants of Budget Deficits in the Industrial Democracies," *European Economic Review* 33 (May, 1989): 903–33.
29. Aleks Szczerbiak, "Interests and Values: Polish Parties and Their Electorates," *Europe-Asia Studies* 51, no. 8 (1999): 1401–32; George Blazyca, "Polish Socioeconomic Development in the 1990s and Scenarios for EU Accession," *Europe-Asia Studies* 51, no. 5 (1999): 799–819.
30. Włodzimierz Puzyna, interview with author, Warsaw, Mar. 6, 2001.
31. Greskovits, *The Political Economy of Protest and Patience,* p. 42.
32. Haggard and Kaufman, "Introduction," p. 17.
33. Ibid., pp. 19–20.
34. Schickler, *Disjointed Pluralism,* p. 268. See also David Braybrooke and C. Lindblom, *The Strategy of Decision: Policy Evaluation as a Social Process;* J. March and H. Simon, *Organizations;* Charles Lindblom, "The Science of Muddling Through," *Public Administration Review* 14 (1959): 79–88; John Kingdon, *Agendas, Alternatives, and Public Policies.*
35. Mitchell Orenstein and Martine Haas, "The Global Politics of Attention and Social Policy Transformation in East-Central Europe."

Chapter 4

1. Michał Kulesza also supports this view. See Kulesza, "Methods and Techniques of Managing Decentralization Reforms," p. 202.
2. Kulesza, *Sprawozdanie z Działalnośći Pełnomocnika,* p. 2, author's translation.
3. Ibid., p. 3, author's translation.
4. Council of Europe, *Charter on Local Government.*
5. Instytut Spraw Publicznych (Institute of Public Affairs), Model Ustrojowy Województwa (Regionu) w Unitarnym Państwie Demokratycznym—Raport Końcowy.
6. Edward Best, "The Maastricht Treaty: What Does it Actually Say and Do," in *The Ratification of the Maastricht Treaty: Issues, Debates, and Future Implications,* ed. F. Laursen and S. Vanhoonacker Dordrecht, p. 25.
7. "The Community shall act within the limits of the powers conferred upon it by this Treaty and of the objectives assigned to it therein. In areas which do not fall within its exclusive competence, the Community shall take action, in accordance with the principle of subsidiarity, only if and in so far as the objectives of the proposed action cannot be sufficiently achieved by the Member States and can therefore, by reason of the scale or effects of the proposed action, be better achieved by the Community. Any action by the Community shall not go beyond what is necessary to achieve the objectives of this Treaty," ibid., p. 25.
8. Gilowska, "Reforma Samorządów a Reforma Finansów Publicznych," p. 23, author's translation.
9. Brusis, "Re-creating the Regional Level in Central and Eastern Europe."
10. EU report 98/701, pp. 9–10, cited in Brusis, "Re-creating the Regional Level in Central and Eastern Europe."
11. This is not to say that the EU did not have a significant influence on the shape of particular aspects of reforms once the decision had been made to undertake them, as demonstrated in the section on provincial reforms.
12. Emilewicz and Wołek, *Reformatorzy i Politycy.*
13. Puzyna interview, July 6, 2000.

14. Jan Maria Rokita, "Samorządowcy, Państwowcy i Psuje," *Panstwo-Rząd-Administracja (Biuletyn Programu Reformy Administracji Publicznej Instytutu Spraw Publicznych)* 7 (Sept., 1998): 1–4.

15. Gilowska, "Reforma Samorządów a Reforma Finansów Publicznych."

16. Małgorzata Strubinska, "Samorządówe Urzędy Pracy," *Wspólnota* 2, no. 513 (2000): 2; Kulesza, "Methods and Techniques of Managing Decentralization Reforms."

17. Counties were also responsible for non-school educational facilities that had been under the auspices of provincial education offices including boarding houses, special education centers, cultural institutions, sport facilities, youth hostels, and psychological and pedagogical advisory centers. Levitas and Herczynski, "Decentralization, Local Governments."

18. Bożena Kołaczek, "Educational Policy of the State," in *Social Policy in the 1990s*, ed. S. Golinowska; Levitas and Herczynski, "Decentralization, Local Governments"; Rokita, "Samorządowcy, Państwowcy i Psuje."

19. In Polish, the Polish Teachers Union is called *Związek Nauczycielstwa Polskiego.*

20. A. Wejner and J. Błędowski, "Krajowy Urząd Pracy Kontra Starostwie: Agonia Form Aktywnych," *Wspólnota* 25, no. 536 (2000): 8–9; Kulesza, "Methods and Techniques of Managing Decentralization Reforms"; Ewa Tomaszewska, interview with author, Warsaw, Sept. 15, 2000; Puzyna interview, July 6, 2000; Michał Kulesza, interview with author, Warsaw, Feb. 15, 2000.

21. Gorzelak and Jałowiecki, *Analiza Procesu Wdrażania.*

22. Rokita, "Samorządowcy, Państwowcy i Psuje," p. 3, author's translation.

23. Kulesza interview, Feb. 15, 2000.

24. Brusis, "Re-creating the Regional Level in Central and Eastern Europe."

25. Gorzelak and Jałowiecki, *Analiza Procesu Wdrażania;* Wollman, "Institution Building and Decentralization in Formerly Socialist Countries."

26. Piekara interview.

27. Ibid.

28. Płoskonka interview.

29. Zaucha, "Regional and Local Development in Poland."

30. Wollman, "Institution Building and Decentralization"; Regulski, *Samorząd III Rzeczypospolitej.*

31. Lipowicz interview.

32. Regulski, *Samorząd III Rzeczypospolitej.*

33. Ibid.

34. Insytut Spraw Publicznych, *Model Ustrojowy Województwa,* p.14, author's translation.

35. Ibid., p. 14, author's translation, emphasis added.

36. Brusis, "Re-creating the Regional Level in Central and Eastern Europe."

37. Insytut Spraw Publicznych, *Model Ustrojowy Województwa,* pp. 22, 24, and 25, author's translation.

38. Ibid.

39. Ibid.

40. Gorzelak and Jałowiecki, *Analiza Procesu Wdrażania;* Jan Maria Rokita, interview with author, Warsaw, Mar. 6, 2001. Rokita was the head of the Institute of Public Affairs, a member of parliament, and a then-influential member of Solidarity Electoral Action (AWS).

41. Levitas, "The Political Economy of Fiscal Decentralization."

42. Puzyna interview, Mar. 6, 2001.

43. Centrum Badania Opinii Społecznej (Public Opinion Research Center), *Korupcja w Życiu Publicznym.*

44. World Bank, *Corruption in Poland: Review of Priority Areas and Proposals for Action.*

45. Open Society Institute, *Monitoring the EU Accession Process: Corruption and Anti-corruption Policy,* p. 404.

46. The project proposed by expert scholars from the University of Warsaw (mentioned previously) also proposed a fewer number of counties; their proposal, however, did not figure into the debate here.

47. Regulski, "Nowy Ustrój, Nowe Szanse, Nowe Problemy."

48. Puzyna interview, July 6, 2000.

49. Emilewicz and Wołek, *Reformatorzy i Politycy.*

50. Ibid.; Regulski, *Samorząd III Rzeczypospolitej;* Lipowicz interview.

51. Gorzelak and Jałowiecki, *Analiza Procesu Wdrażania;* Janik interview.

52. Emilewicz and Wołek, *Reformatorzy i Politycy;* Gorzelak and Jałowiecki, *Analiza Procesu Wdrażania.*

53. Sekuła interview.

54. Ibid.

55. Seven new counties were added to this number on January 1, 2002. H. Miklaszewska, "Radość Nowych Powiatów," *Wspólnota* 23, no. 587 (2001): 23.

56. Gorzelak and Jałowiecki, *Analiza Procesu Wdrażania;* MSWiA (Polish Ministry of Internal Affairs and Administration), *Powiaty i Miasta na Prawach Powiatu po Roku Reformy.*

57. G. Gorzelak and B. Jałowiecki, "Reforma Terytorialnej Organizacji Kraju: Wnioski po Dwóch Latach," in *Reforma Terytorialnej Organizacji Kraju: Dwa Lata Doświadczeń,* ed. G. Gorzelak, B. Jałowiecki, and M. Stec, p. 23, author's translation.

58. Most of the research and work on the number of provinces was conducted in the Center for Social and Economic Research (CASE), a Polish think tank. Gorzelak and Jałowiecki, *Analiza Procesu Wdrażania.*

59. Regulski, *Samorząd III Rzeczypospolitej.*

60. Insytut Spraw Publicznych, *Model Ustrojowy Województwa.*

61. EU avis 97/7, p. 72, cited in Brusis, "Re-creating the Regional Level in Central and Eastern Europe."

62. Brusis, "Re-creating the Regional Level in Central and Eastern Europe"; Insytut Spraw Publicznych, *Model Ustrojowy Województwa;* Rokita interview.

63. Puzyna interview, July 6, 2000.

64. Ibid.

65. Levitas, "The Political Economy of Fiscal Decentralization."

66. Emilewicz and Wołek, *Reformatorzy i Politycy.*

67. Ibid., Michał Kulesza, interview with author, Warsaw, June 27, 2000.

68. Gorzelak and Jałowiecki, "Reforma Terytorialnej Organizacji Kraju."

69. Beata Gadomska, "Die Neugliederung der Offentlichen Verwaltung in Polen," in *Central and Eastern Europe on the Way into the European Union,* ed. E. von Breska and M. Brusis.

70. For example, a 1997 EU country assessment for Poland noted that local government in Poland lacked sufficient financial resources for it to operate autonomously from the central government. EU avis 97/7, p. 17, cited in Brusis, "Re-creating the Regional Level in Central and Eastern Europe."

71. Sekuła interview.

72. No evidence was found that these international organizations directly influenced the behavior of Balcerowicz or Miller with regard to the reform.

73. Levitas, "The Political Economy of Fiscal Decentralization," p. 50.

74. Sekuła interview.

75. Tony Levitas, interview with author, Warsaw, June 20, 2001.

76. Levitas, "The Political Economy of Fiscal Decentralization"; Kulesza, *Sprawozdanie z Działalnośći Pełnomocnika.*

77. There was also a fear that giving such tax collection authority to subnational levels would go against Poland's principle of a unitary state. Levitas interview.

78. Danuta Wawrzynkiewicz, interview with author, Warsaw, June 19, 2001.

79. Levitas interview.

80. Wawrzynkiewicz interview.

81. Levitas interview.

82. Ibid.; Wawrzynkiewicz interview.

83. Levitas, "The Political Economy of Fiscal Decentralization," p. 43.

84. Ibid.

85. Puzyna interview, July 6, 2000; Sekuła interview.

86. Józef Płoskonka, "Główne Założenia," in *Cztery Reformy,* ed. L. Kolarska-Bobinska.

87. Kulesza, *Sprawozdanie z Działalnośći Pełnomocnika,* p. 32, author's translation.

88. Puzyna interview, July 6, 2000; Sekuła interview.

89. Kulesza, *Sprawozdanie z Działalnośći Pełnomocnika.*

90. An interview with Jerzy Miller indicates that he may have apparently felt justified in his approach because he thought he was doing what was best for the country as a whole, even if it meant circumventing the participation of others in the process.

91. Puzyna interview, Mar. 6, 2001; Kulesza, *Sprawozdanie z Działalnośći Pełnomocnika.*

92. Emilewicz and Wołek, *Reformatorzy i Politycy;* Puzyna interview, Mar. 6, 2001.

93. Kulesza interview, Feb. 15, 2000; Emilewicz and Wołek, *Reformatorzy i Politycy;* Sekuła interview.

94. Związek Powiatów Polskich (Association of Polish Counties), *Monitorowanie Działalności Powiatów Polskich—Raport 1.*

95. Gorzelak and Jałowiecki, *Analiza Procesu Wdrażania.*

96. Maria Weber, "Nowy Rok—Stare Kłopoty," *Wspólnota* 52–53, no. 563–64 (2000): 38–39; Jędrzejewska, "Samorządowcy Mają Inny Pomysł na Dochody"; Małgorzata Strubinska, "Proteza Zamiast Ustawy," *Wspólnota* 31, no. 542 (2000): 9.

97. Związek Powiatów Polskich (Association of Polish Counties), *Monitorowanie Działalności Powiatów.*

98. Weber, "Nowy Rok—Stare Kłopoty." There is a large question about whether or not fiscal decentralization will solve this problem for the many small counties created with the reform, because their small tax bases would limit the amount of revenue they could generate. They would therefore either still be dependent on the central government for equalizing transfers, or their limited funds would inhibit democracy.

Chapter 5

1. Some reference is made to secondary effects of the reform to the municipal level in the area of social service delivery though the reform did not legally alter municipal legislation.

2. Zaucha, "Regional and Local Development in Poland," p. 75.

3. Chancellory of the President of the Council of Ministers, *Ogólne Założenia Reformy Ustrojowej Państwa,* p. 25, author's translation.
4. The legal mandate was established by the 1990 Law on Social Welfare.
5. Homes for the elderly are similar to residential nursing homes in the United States but for more diverse populations.
6. Decentralization at the municipal level occurred with Poland's first administrative reform in 1990, which also provided for democratic elections in municipalities.
7. Emilewicz and Wołek, *Reformatorzy i Politycy.*
8. Dziennik Ustaw, "Ustawa o Zmianie Niektórych Ustaw Związanych z Funkcjonowaniem Administracji Publicznej," *Dziennik Ustaw Rzeczypospolitej Polskiej,* Nr 12, poz. 136, 21 styczeń 2000.
9. T. Każmierczak and A. Olech, *Wstępny Raport o Sytuacji Centrów Pomocy Rodzinie Działających w Powiatach Ziemskich.*
10. J. Hrynkiewicz et al., *Raport z Realizacji Projektu Badawczego Zadania Społeczne Powiatu dla Ministerstwa Spraw Wewnętrznych i Administracji.*
11. Najwyższa Izba Kontroli (Polish State Auditing Office), *Informacja o Wynikach Kontroli Realizacji Zadań w 1999r. z Zakresu Pomocy Społecznej przez Jednostki Samorządu Terytorialnego.*
12. The sample for county family assistance centers was stratified according to two types of counties: counties that encircle cities with county status (46) and remaining "regular" counties (262). Thirty-three counties of each type were randomly sampled and survey results weighted according to their actual numbers when data from the two types of counties were combined.
13. One exception was a survey that was mailed to a county director and then faxed back in return.
14. Fowler, *Survey Research Methods.*
15. Funding was provided by a Fulbright-Hays Dissertation Research Abroad Fellowship 1999–2000.
16. Harry Hatry, *Performance Measurement: Getting Results.*
17. Grosse supports this view. He states, "Due to the meagerness of 'own' resources and financial dependency on the central government, the county becomes a subcontractor and administrator of social service tasks. Although it possesses significant financial resources, in practice, it has no influence on the way they are spent. As a result, a side effect of such a systemic and financial construction is the limiting of county initiative, reducing the desire of local government actors to participate in social policy programming." See Tomasz Grzegorz Grosse, "Polityka Społeczna w Samorządzie Terytorialnym," *Samorząd Terytorialny* 4 (2003): 50, author's translation.
18. Związek Powiatów Polskich (Association of Polish Counties), *Monitorowanie Działalności Powiatów Polskich;* A. Orzechowski, "Niedokończona Reforma," *Wspólnota* 52–53, no. 563–64 (2000): 20–21.
19. Levitas and Herczynski, "Decentralization, Local Governments." Fiscal decentralization in Poland and Europe generally includes both the transfer of revenue-generating authority to lower levels and any funds subnational governments are given that they are free to spend as they choose. This includes subnational government shares in PIT and CIT (collected and disbursed on the central level) not earmarked for specific purposes by the central government.
20. The exact survey question asked with regard to need was, "According to you [the director] to what degree did central government and local government funds cover need in the area of the following tasks—0%, 25%, 50%, 75%, 100%?" Admittedly this was a very subjective and imprecise way of determining need; however, the purpose of the question was to establish large differences in funding between different types and kinds of social service tasks and between regular counties and cities with county status. In general the

intent of the survey was to uncover broad trends in a number of different areas, an approach that precludes a detailed evaluation of any one area.

County funds covered 16 percent of need for specialist counseling, 6 percent of need for operating a crisis intervention center, and 63 percent of need for help with integration for youth leaving institutions.

21. For example, city funds covered 53 percent of need for specialist counseling, 41 percent of need for operating a crisis intervention center, and 63 percent of need for help with integration (this last percentage matches the county figure).

22. Some tasks are between being a commissioned and a county task; that is, formally they are considered county tasks but they are still being funded directly by the central government. In some cases where the commissioned task involves the use of an institution (i.e., social assistance homes) only those counties and cities that "inherited" these structures with the reform receive funding in this area and thus can implement these services. For these reasons, both of these types of tasks were omitted from the present analysis.

23. Broken down by task, central government funds covered 98 percent of need for financial aid to foster children, 91 percent of need for financial aid for youth leaving institutions, and 74 percent of need in salaries for county workers.

24. By task, central government funds covered 92 percent of need for financial aid to foster children, 80 percent of need for financial aid to youth leaving institutions, and 57 percent of need for county workers' salaries.

25. This disparity may possibly be due to a difference in county and city directors' perceptions of need in their area for services.

26. Hrynkiewicz, *Raport z Realizacji;* Związek Powiatów Polskich (Association of Polish Counties), *Monitorowanie Działalności Powiatów Polskich;* Najwyższa Izba Kontroli, (Polish State Auditing Office), *Informacja o Wynikach;* Polish State Auditing Office report cited in Beata Kalinowska, "Najbardziej Potrzebujący bez Wsparcia" *Wspólnota* 49, no. 613 (2001): 38–39; Ewa Leś, L. Kozaczuk, T. Malachowska, and M. Sodel, "Cele i Skuteczność Reformy Administracji Publicznej w RP w Latach 1999–2001 w Dziedzinie Pomocy Społecznej—Synteza Badań."

27. The survey asked to what percentage did funds cover need in 1999 while degree of task implementation was determined for summer, 2000, the time of the survey. Funding patterns did not change significantly in 2000.

28. This number hides significant variation between tasks. For example, 28 percent of counties indicated they have fully implemented specialist counseling, only 15 percent are operating a crisis intervention center, and 42 percent provide help with integration for youth leaving institutions.

29. This number is reflected in the percentages for individual tasks: 61 percent have fully implemented specialist counseling, 55 percent operate a crisis intervention center, and a full 75 percent provide help with integration.

30. Eighty-eight percent provide financial aid for foster children, 81 percent provide financial aid for youth leaving institutions, and 59 percent pay salaries for county workers.

One-hundred percent provide financial aid for foster children, 96 percent provide financial aid for youth leaving institutions, and 74 percent provide salaries for county workers.

31. Kaźmierczak and Olech, *Wstępny Raport.*

32. Z. Kuzmiuk, "Mazowsze Negocjuje Kontrakt," *Wspólnota* 15, no. 579 (2001): 26–27.

33. Grosse, "Polityka Społeczna w Samorządzie," p. 49, author's translation.

34. Koral, "Sukcesy i Porażki Wdrażanej Reformy," p. 55, author's translation.

35. Only 6 percent said it was better, and 5 percent said they did not know. The response to this survey question is dependent on directors' memory of the situation before the reform, which may have introduced some inconsistencies.

36. Hrynkiewicz, *Raport z Realizacji.*

37. Grosse, "Polityka Społeczna w Samorządzie," p. 50, author's translation.

38. Maria Tkaczyk also makes this assertion in "Zespoły Orzekające o Stopniu Niepełnosprawności," in *Raport z Realizacji Projektu Badawczego Zadania Społeczne Powiatu dla Ministerstwa Spraw Wewnętrznych i Administracji,* J. Hrynkiewicz et al.

39. Czesław Martysz, "Właściwość Organów Samorządu Terytorialnego do Wydawania Decyzji Administracyjnych w Sprawach Pomocy Społecznej," *Samorząd Terytorialnego* 1–2, no.109–10 (2000): 91–101. This is most evident in laws governing the funding of services for the disabled, which reserve the right for the county head to make financial decisions regarding these matters (Szarek, 2000).

40. Seventeen percent of these had worked previously in the old provincial social assistance office.

41. I. Baczak, "Bohaterowie są Zmęczeni," *Wspólnota* 41, no. 552 (2000): 5–6.

42. Social assistance homes *(domy pomocy społecznej)* are residential institutions for the elderly, chronically ill, developmentally disabled, physically disabled, long-term mentally ill, and single mothers who are pregnant or have small children. See Lidia Ulanowska, "Domy Pomocy Społecznej," in *Raport z Realizacji Projektu Badawczego Zadania Społeczne Powiatu dla Ministerstwa Spraw Wewnętrznych i Administracji,* J. Hrynkiewicz et al.

43. Levitas, "The Political Economy of Fiscal Decentralization."

44. J. Duda, J. Modzelewski, and W. Skiba, *Pomoc Społeczna—Raport Końcowy.*

45. Ibid.

46. Ibid.

47. Accessibility here means how quickly a prospective recipient is able to receive services.

48. Six percent said they did not know.

49. Eleven percent did not know or left the question blank.

50. The response to this survey question is also dependent on directors' memory of the situation before the reform, which may have introduced some inconsistencies.

51. Puzyna interview, July 6, 2000.

52. Kulesza interview, Feb. 15, 2000; Każmierczak and Olech, *Wstępny Raport.*

53. Każmierczak and Olech, *Wstępny Raport.*

54. Ustawa z dnia 29 listopada 1990r. o pomocy społecznej [Law of November 29, 1990, on social welfare]. Dz.U.98.64.414 zm. Dz.U.00.19.238.

55. The nine tasks considered were provision of information regarding legal rights, specialist counseling, realization of tasks of the National Fund for the Rehabilitation of the Disabled, operating county support centers for the mentally ill, organizing care in foster families, operating a crisis intervention center, developing a county strategy for solving social problems, help with integration for youth leaving institutions, and operating youth rehabilitation centers.

    These numbers hide significant variation among the nine tasks on which they are based. For example, the task of providing information on legal rights is contracted out by 5 percent of centers and subsidized by 3 percent, while some type of informal cooperation involving this task occurs in 48 percent of centers. By contrast, the task of operating county support centers for the mentally ill is contracted out by only 1 percent, subsidized by 2 percent, and sees informal cooperation by only 10 percent of centers.

56. J. J. Wygnański, "Elementy Budowania i Uczęstnictwa w Programach Współpracy Organizacji Pozarządowych z Administracją Publiczną" *Roczniak* 4, (1998): 15–34.

57. Grzegorz Roczek, "Nauka o Powiatach," *Wspólnota* 10, no. 626 (2002): 56. For a discussion on difficulties for NGO development in a transitioning environment based on a case study of Poland see Joanna Regulska, "NGOs and their Vulnerabilities during the Time of Transition: The Case of Poland," *Voluntas: International Journal of Voluntary and Nonprofit Organizations* 10, no. 1 (1999): 61–71.

58. These figures are consistent with those found in the Ministry of Labor and Social Policy commissioned report in Każmierczak and Olech, *Wstępny Raport.*
59. Some of these figures varied significantly between counties and cities.
60. Disability eligibility offices were excluded.
61. Hrynkiewicz, *Raport z Realizacji*; Leś, Kozaczuk, Malachowska, and Sodel, "Cele i Skuteczność Reformy Administracji Publicznej."

Chapter 6

1. Haggard and Kaufman, "Introduction." See also Greskovits, *The Political Economy of Protest and Patience* for a discussion on economic reformers in transitioning countries who fail to consult and negotiate with outside actors and use secrecy to achieve their ends.
2. Lindblom in particular addresses this "flying by the seat of one's pants" method of policy-making in Lindblom, "The Science of Muddling Through."
3. Admittedly, there are other possible categories to this model such as contested-uninformed and others. The categories found here were developed according to that political factor that had an overriding effect on policy outcomes. Therefore, some categories were not included because, for example, with the category "contested politics," the effect of contested politics outweighed that of uninformed politics.
4. The Ministry of Labor and Social Policy was, however, successful in stalling the decentralization of labor offices and other labor policy.
5. Paul Appleby, *Policy and Administration,* p. 97.
6. Kirchner and Christiansen make this point about value judgments and add the important fact that they change over time in Kirchner and Christiansen, "The Importance of Local and Regional Reform."
7. Francis Conway, B. Desilets, P. Epstein, and J. Pigey, *Sourcebook on Intergovernmental Fiscal Relations in Eastern Europe,* p. 14.
8. J. Litvak, J. Ahmad, and R. Bird, *Rethinking Decentralization in Developing Countries,* p. 25. The soufflé comparison is attributed to Andrew N. Parker, *Decentralization: The Way Forward for Rural Development?*
9. Greskovits, *The Political Economy of Protest and Patience,* p. 181.
10. Kingdon, *Agendas, Alternatives, and Public Policies.*
11. Kirchner and Christiansen, "The Importance of Local and Regional Reform," p. 16.

Bibliography

Alesina, Alberto. "Political Models of Macroeconomic Policy and Fiscal Reforms." In *Voting for Reform: Democracy, Political Liberalization, and Economic Adjustment,* edited by S. Haggard and S. Webb. New York: Published for the World Bank, Oxford University Press, 1994.

Allard, S. "Revisiting Shapiro: Welfare Magnets and State Residency Requirements in the 1990s." *Publius* 28, no. 3 (1998): 45–65.

Appleby, Paul. *Policy and Administration.* University: University of Alabama Press, 1949.

Baczak, I. "Bohaterowie są Zmęczeni." *Wspólnota* 41, no. 552 (2000): 5–6.

Beck, C. H. *Samorząd Terytorialny.* Warsaw: Wydawnictwo C. H. Beck, 1999.

Best, Edward. "The Maastricht Treaty: What Does It Actually Say and Do." In *The Ratification of the Maastricht Treaty: Issues, Debates, and Future Implications,* edited by F. Laursen and S. Vanhoonacker Dordrecht. The Netherlands: Martinus Nijhoff Publishers, 1994.

Bird, R., R. Ebel, and C. Wallich. "Fiscal Decentralization: From Command to Market." In *Decentralization of the Socialist State,* edited by R. Bird, R. Ebel, and C. Wallich. Washington, D.C.: The World Bank, 1995.

Blair, Harry. "Participation and Accountability at the Periphery: Democratic Local Governance in Six Countries." *World Development* 28, no. 1 (2000): 21–39.

Blazyca, George. "Polish Socioeconomic Development in the 1990s and Scenarios for EU Accession." *Europe-Asia Studies* 51, no. 5 (1999): 799–819.

Bonoli, Giuliano. *The Politics of Pension Reform: Institutions and Policy Change in Western Europe.* Cambridge: Cambridge University Press, 2000.

Braybrooke, David, and C. Lindblom. *The Strategy of Decision: Policy Evaluation as a Social Process.* New York: Free Press of Glencoe, 1963.

Brusis, Martin. "Re-creating the Regional Level in Central and Eastern Europe: An Analysis of Administrative Reforms in Six Countries." In *Central and Eastern Europe on the Way into the European Union: Reforms of Regional Administration in Bulgaria, the Czech Republic, Estonia, Hungary, Poland and Slovakia,* edited by Erik von Breska and Martin Brusis. Munich: Center for Applied Policy Research, 1999.

Bunce, Valerie. "The Political Economy of Postsocialism." *Slavic Review* 58, no. 4 (1999): 756–93.

Cain, Michael, and Aleksander Surdej. "Transitional Politics or Public Choice? Evaluating Stalled Pension Reforms in Poland." In *Left Parties and Social Policy in Postcommunist Europe,* edited by L. Cook, M. Orenstein, and M. Rueschemeyer. Boulder, Colo.: Westview Press, 1999.

Cameron, D., and R. Hofferbert. "The Impact of Federalism on Education Finance: A Comparative Analysis." *European Journal of Political Research* 2 (September, 1974): 225–58.

Centrum Badania Opinii Społecznej (Public Opinion Research Center). *Korupcja w Życiu Publicznym.* Warsaw: CBOS, 1999.

Chancellory of the President of the Council of Ministers. *Ogólne Założenia Reformy Ustrojowej Państwa.* Warsaw: Department of State Systemic Reform, Chancellory of the President of the Council of Ministers, May, 1998.

Chancellory of the Prime Minister. *Effectiveness, Openness, Subsidiarity: A New Poland for New Challenges.* Warsaw: Chancellory of the Prime Minister of the Republic of Poland, Government Plenipotentiary for the Systemic Reform of the State, December, 1998.

Chancellory of the Sejm. *The Constitution of the Republic of Poland.* Warsaw: Sejm Publishing Office, 1997.

Conway, Francis, B. Desilets, P. Epstein, and J. Pigey. *Sourcebook on Intergovernmental Fiscal Relations in Eastern Europe.* Washington, D.C.: The Urban Institute, 2001. (Prepared for USAID and World Bank Institute)

Council of Europe. *Charter on Local Government.* Retrieved from http://conventions.coe.int/Treaty/en/Treaties/Html/122.htm., 1991.

Czubaszek, B., ed. *Ustrój Administracji Przepisów: Zbiór Najnowszych Przepisów.* Warsaw: Wydawnictwo Prawno-Ekonomiczne INFOR, 1999.

Dahl, Robert. *Dilemmas of Pluralist Democracy: Autonomy vs. Control.* New Haven, Conn.: Yale University Press, 1982.

Davies, Norman. *God's Playground: A History of Poland. Vol I. The Origins to 1795.* New York: Columbia University Press, 1982.

———. *God's Playground: A History of Poland. Vol II. 1795 to the Present.* New York: Columbia University Press, 1982.

Duda, J., J. Modzelewski, and W. Skiba. *Pomoc Społeczna—Raport Końcowy.* Wrocław: Wrocławska Agencja Rozwoju Regionalnego S.A., 1999.

Dziennik Ustaw. "Ustawa o Zmianie Niektórych Ustaw Związanych z Funkcjonowaniem Administracji Publicznej." *Dziennik Ustaw Rzeczypospolitej Polskiej* [Journal of Laws of the Republic of Poland], Nr 12, poz. 136, 21 styczeń 2000.

Eaton, Kent. "Fiscal Decentralization in Developing Democracies: What's at Stake for Legislators?" Paper presented at the Yale Colloquium on Decentralization and Development, October, 1999.

Emilewicz, Jadwiga, and Artur Wołek. *Reformatorzy i Politycy.* Warsaw: Fundacja Rozwoju Demokracji Lokalnej, 2000.

Faguet, Jean-Paul. *Does Decentralization Increase Responsiveness to Local Needs? Evidence from Bolivia.* Working Paper. Washington, D.C.: World Bank, 2000.

Fenrych, P., and W. Puzyna. "Wielka Decentralizacja." *Więź* 6, no. 512 (2001): 14–28.

Fowler, Floyd. *Survey Research Methods.* Newbury Park, Calif.: Sage Publications, 1993.

Gadomska, Beata. "Die Neugliederung der Öffentlichen Verwaltung in Polen."

In *Central and Eastern Europe on the Way into the European Union: Reforms of Regional Administration in Bulgaria, the Czech Republic, Estonia, Hungary, Poland and Slovakia,* edited by E. von Breska and M. Brusis. Munich: Center for Applied Policy Research, 1999.

Gilowska, Zyta. "Reforma Samorządów a Reforma Finansów Publicznych." In *Cztery Reformy: Od Koncepcji do Realizacji,* edited by Lena Kolarska-Bobinska. Warsaw: Oficyna Naukowa, 2000.

Giugale, M. and S. Webb, eds., *Achievements and Challenges of Fiscal Decentralization: Lessons from Mexico.* Washington, D.C.: The World Bank, 2000.

Gorzelak, G. "Decentralization, Regional Development and Regional Policies." In *Poland into the New Millennium,* edited by G. Blazyca and R. Rapacki. Northampton, Mass.: Edward Elgar, 2001.

Gorzelak, G., and B. Jałowiecki. *Analiza Procesu Wdrażania i Skutków Reformy Terytorialnej Organizacji Kraju—Raport Końcowy.* Warsaw: Europejski Instytut Rozwoju Regionalnego i Lokalnego and Instytut Spraw Publicznych, 2001.

———. "Reforma Terytorialnej Organizacji Kraju: Wnioski po Dwóch Latach." In *Reforma Terytorialnej Organizacji Kraju: Dwa Lata Doświadczeń,* edited by G. Gorzelak, B. Jałowiecki, and M. Stec. Warsaw: Wydawnictwo Naukowe "Scholar," 2001.

Greskovits, Béla. *The Political Economy of Protest and Patience.* Budapest: Central European University Press, 1998.

Grochowski, M., and J. Regulska. "New Partnership and Collaboration: Local Government and Its Supporting Institutions—The Case of Poland." In *Towards a New Concept of Local Self-Government?,* edited by Erik Amna and Stig Montin. Poland: Fagbokforlaget, 2000.

Grosse, Tomasz Grzegorz. "Polityka Społeczna w Samorządzie Terytorialnym." *Samorząd Terytorialny* 4 (2003): 48–59.

Haggard, Stephan, and Robert Kaufman. *The Political Economy of Democratic Transitions.* Princeton: Princeton University Press, 1995.

Haggard, Stephan, and Robert Kaufman. "Introduction." In *Reforming the State: Fiscal and Welfare Reform in Post-Socialist Countries,* edited by J. Kornai, S. Haggard, and R. Kaufman. Cambridge: Cambridge University Press, 2001.

Haggard, Stephan, and S. B. Webb. "Introduction." In *Voting for Reform: Democracy, Political Liberalization, and Economic Adjustment,* edited by S. Haggard and S. B. Webb. New York: Oxford University Press, 1994.

Hatry, Harry. *Performance Measurement: Getting Results.* Washington, D.C.: The Urban Institute Press, 1999.

Hesse, Joachim J. "Rebuilding the State: Public Sector Reform in Central and Eastern Europe." In *Public Sector Reform: Rationale, Trends and Problems,* edited by Jan-Erik Lane. London: Sage, 1997.

Horvath, Tamas M., ed. *Decentralization: Experiments and Reforms.* Budapest: Local Government and Public Service Reform Initiative/Open Society Institute, 2000.

Hrynkiewicz, J. et al. *Raport z Realizacji Projektu Badawczego Zadania Społeczne Powiatu dla Ministerstwa Spraw Wewnętrznych i*

Administracji. Warsaw: Institute of Applied Social Sciences, University of Warsaw, 1999.

Huntington, Samuel. *The Third Wave: Democratisation in the Late 20th Century.* Tulsa: University of Oklahoma Press, 1991.

Huther, J., and A. Shah. *Applying a Simple Measure of Good Governance to the Debate on Fiscal Decentralization.* Working Paper No. 1894. Washington, D.C.: World Bank, 1998.

Illner, Michal. "Territorial Decentralization—A Stumbling Block of Democratic Reforms in East-Central Europe?" *Polish Sociological Review* 1, no. 117 (1997): 23–45.

Instytut Spraw Publicznych (Institute of Public Affairs). *Model Ustrojowy Województwa (Regionu) w Unitarnym Państwie Demokratycznym—Raport Końcowy.* Warsaw: Instytut Spraw Publicznych, 1997.

Izdebski, Hubert. *Samorząd Terytorialny: Podstawy Ustroju i Działalności.* Warsaw: Wydawnictwo Prawnicze LexisNexis, 2003.

———. "Samorząd Terytorialny w II Rzeczypospolitej." In *Samorząd Terytorialny: Zagadnienia Prawne i Administracyjne,* edited by Andrzej Piekara and Zygmunt Niewiadomski. Warsaw: Wydawnictwo Prawnicze, 1998.

Janik, Krzysztof (deputy chair, Polish parliamentary committee on local government and regional policy; secretary general, Democratic Left Alliance party). Interview with author. Warsaw, July 19, 2000.

Jędrzejewska, Katarzyna. "Samorządowcy Mają Inny Pomysł na Dochody." *Rzeczpospolita,* May 26, 2000.

Johnson, S., and M. Kowalska. "Poland: The Political Economy of Shock Therapy." In *Voting for Reform: Democracy, Political Liberalization, and Economic Adjustment,* edited by S. Haggard and S. B. Webb. New York: Oxford University Press, 1994.

Kalinowska, Beata. "Najbardziej Potrzebujący bez Wsparcia." *Wspólnota* 49, no. 613 (2001): 38–39.

Kaminski, M., G. Lissowski, and P. Swistak. "The 'Revival of Communism' or the Effect of Institutions? The 1993 Polish Parliamentary Elections." *Public Choice* 97, no. 3 (1998): 429–50.

Kaźmierczak, T., and A. Olech. *Wstępny Raport o Sytuacji Centrów Pomocy Rodzinie Działających w Powiatach Ziemskich.* Warsaw: Ministry of Labor and Social Policy, 1999.

Kettl, D. *Reinventing Government? Appraising the National Performance Review.* Washington, D.C.: The Brookings Institution, 1994.

Kingdon, John. *Agendas, Alternatives, and Public Policies.* New York: HarperCollins College Publishers, 1995.

Kirchner, E., ed. *Decentralization and Transition in the Visegrad.* New York: St. Martin's Press, 1999.

Kirchner, E., and T. Christiansen. "The Importance of Local and Regional Reform." In *Decentralization and Transition in the Visegrad,* edited by E. Kirchner. New York: St. Martin's Press, 1999.

Kołaczek, Bożena. "Educational Policy of the State." In *Social Policy in the 1990s,* edited by S. Golinowska. Warsaw: IPiSS, 1998.

Kolarska-Bobinska, Lena. "Wstęp." In *Cztery Reformy: Od Koncepcji do Realizacji,* edited by L. Kolarska-Bobinska. Warsaw: Oficyna Naukowa, 2000.

Koral, Jolanta. "Sukcesy i Porażki Wdrażanej Reformy." In *Cztery Reformy: Od Koncepcji do Realizacji,* edited by L. Kolarska-Bobinska. Warsaw: Oficyna Naukowa, 2000.

Kowalczyk, Andrzej. "Local Government in Poland." In *Decentralization: Experiments and Reforms,* edited by T. Horvath. Budapest: Local Government and Public Service Reform Initiative/Open Society Institute, 2000.

Kuklinski, Antoni, and P. Swianiewicz. "The Polish Palatinatus: Experiences and Prospects." In *The Rise of Meso Government in Europe,* edited by L. J. Sharpe. London: Sage Publications, 1993.

Kulesza, Michał (former secretary of state and government plenipotentiary for state structural reforms, 1997–99). Interview with author. Warsaw, February 15, 2000.

———. Interview with Author. Warsaw, June 27, 2000.

———. "Methods and Techniques of Managing Decentralization Reforms in CEE Countries: The Polish Experience." In *Mastering Decentralization and Public Administration Reforms in Central and Eastern Europe,* edited by Gábor Péteri. Budapest: Local Government and Public Service Reform Initiative/Open Society Institute, 2002.

———. *Sprawozdanie z Działalnośći Pełnomocnika Rządu ds. Reform Ustrojowych Państwa.* Government document, March, 1999.

Kutyla, Dorota, ed. *Zasadniczy Trójstopniowy Podział Terytorialny Polski: Komentarz do Przepisów.* Warsaw: Twigger, 1999.

Kuzmiuk, Z. "Mazowsze Negocjuje Kontrakt." *Wspólnota* 15, no. 579 (2001): 26–27.

Leś, Ewa. "Zasada Subsydiarność i jej Użyteczność w Reformowaniu Instytucji Pomocy Społecznej w Polsce." Unpublished Paper, 1998. In author's possession.

Leś, Ewa, L. Kozaczuk, T. Malachowska, and M. Sodel. "Cele i Skuteczność Reformy Administracji Publicznej w RP w Latach 1999–2001 w Dziedzinie Pomocy Społecznej—Synteza Badań." Unpublished Report, 2002.

Levitas, Tony (former USAID expert advisor to Jerzy Miller, the undersecretary of state for fiscal decentralization, Ministry of Finance). Interview with author. Warsaw, June 20, 2001.

———. "The Political Economy of Fiscal Decentralization and Local Government Finance Reform in Poland." Paper prepared for USAID, 1999.

Levitas, Tony, and Jan Herczynski. "Decentralization, Local Governments and Education Reform in Post-Communist Poland." Paper prepared for the Open Society Institute's Local Government Initiative Program, 2001.

Lijphart, A. *Democracies: Pattern of Majoritarian and Consensus Government in Twenty-one Countries.* New Haven: Yale University Press, 1984.

Lindblom, Charles E. "The Science of Muddling Through." *Public Administration Review* 14 (1959): 79–88.

Linz, Juan. J., and Alfred Stepan. *Problems of Democratic Transition and Consolidation: South America and Post-Communist Europe.* Baltimore: Johns Hopkins University Press, 1996.

Lipowicz, Irena (former chair, Polish parliamentary committee on local government and regional policy; member, Freedom Union party). Interview with author. Vienna, August 7, 2000.

Litvak, J., J. Ahmad, and R. Bird. *Rethinking Decentralization in Developing Countries.* Washington, D.C.: The World Bank, 1988.

Luong, P. J. "The Path Least Resisted: The Politics of Economic Decentralization in Kazakhstan." Paper presented at the Yale Colloquium on Decentralization and Development, March, 2000.

Manor, James. *The Political Economy of Democratic Decentralization.* Washington, D.C.: The World Bank, 1999.

March, J., and H. Simon. *Organizations.* New York: Wiley, 1958.

Martysz, Czesław. "Właściwość Organów Samorządu Terytorialnego do Wydawania Decyzji Administracyjnych w Sprawach Pomocy Społecznej." *Samorząd Terytorialnego* 1–2, no.109–10 (2000): 91–101.

Mettler, Suzanne. *Dividing Citizens: Gender and Federalism in New Deal Public Policy.* Ithaca: Cornell University Press, 1998.

Miklaszewska, H. "Radość Nowych Powiatów." *Wspólnota* 23, no. 587 (2001): 23.

Ministerstwo Spraw Wewnętrznych i Administracji (MSWiA; Polish Ministry of Internal Affairs and Administration). *Powiaty i Miasta na Prawach Powiatu po Roku Reformy.* Ministry report, 2000.

Najwyższa Izba Kontroli (Polish State Auditing Office). *Informacja o Wynikach Kontroli Realizacji Zadań w 1999r. z Zakresu Pomocy Społecznej przez Jednostki Samorządu Terytorialnego.* Warsaw: Department of Labor and Social Affairs, State Auditing Office, 2000.

Nathan, R., and T. Gais. "Early Findings about the Newest New Federalism for Welfare." *Publius* 28, no. 3 (1998): 95–103.

North, Douglass. *Institutions, Institutional Change, and Economic Performance.* Cambridge: Cambridge University Press, 1990.

Nunberg, B., and L. Barbone. "Breaking Administrative Deadlock in Poland: Internal Obstacles and External Incentives." In *The State after Communism: Administrative Transitions in Central and Eastern Europe,* edited by B. Nunberg. Washington, D.C.: The World Bank, 1999.

Oakerson, Ronald J. *Governing Local Public Economies.* Oakland, Calif.: ICS Press, 1999.

Olson, Mancur. "The Devolution of Power in Post-Communist Societies: Therapies for Corruption, Fragmentation and Economic Retardation." In *Russia's Stormy Path to Reform,* edited by R. Skidelsky. London: Social Market Foundation, 1995.

Open Society Institute. *Monitoring the EU Accession Process: Corruption and Anti-corruption Policy.* Budapest: Open Society Institute, EU Accession Monitoring Program, 2002.

Orenstein, Mitchell. *Out of the Red: Building Capitalism and Democracy in Postcommunist Europe.* Ann Arbor: University of Michigan Press, 2001.

Orenstein, Mitchell, and Martine Haas. "The Global Politics of Attention and Social Policy Transformation in East-Central Europe." Conference paper presented at the Annual Meeting of the American Association for the Advancement of Slavic Studies, 2000.

Orzechowski, A. "Niedokończona Reforma." *Wspólnota* 52–53, no. 563–64 (2000): 20–21.

Osborne, D., and T. Gaebler. *Reinventing Government.* New York: The Penguin Group, 1992.

Osmani, S. R. *Participatory Governance, People's Empowerment and Poverty Reduction.* New York: United Nations Development Program, Social Development and Poverty Elimination Division, SEPED Conference Paper No. 7, 2000.

Ostrom, Elinor. "Metropolitan Reform: Propositions Derived from Two Traditions." *Social Science Quarterly* 53 (1972): 474–93.

Ostrom, Vincent, R. Bish, and E. Ostrom. *Local Government in the United States.* San Francisco: ICS Press, 1988.

Parker, Andrew N. *Decentralization: The Way forward for Rural Development?* Policy Research Working Paper No. 1475. Washington, D.C.: World Bank, 1995.

Peterson, P. *The Price of Federalism.* Washington, D.C.: Brookings Institution, 1995.

Piekara, Andrzej (director, Center for Local Government and Development, University of Warsaw). Interview with author. Warsaw, March 6, 2001.

Pierson, Paul. "Increasing Returns, Path Dependence, and the Study of Politics." Typescript, Howard University, 1998.

Płoskonka, Józef. "Główne Założenia." In *Cztery Reformy: Od Koncepcji do Realizacji,* edited by Lena Kolarska-Bobinska. Warsaw: Oficyna Naukowa, 2000.

——— (secretary of state, Ministry of Internal Affairs and Administration; researcher, Institute of Public Affairs). Interview with author. Warsaw, March 8, 2001.

———. *Reforma Administracji Publicznej, 1998–2001.* Warsaw: Ministry of Internal Affairs and Administration, 2001.

Prud'homme, Remy. "On the Dangers of Decentralization." *The World Bank Research Observer* 10, no. 2 (1995): 201–10.

Przeworksi, Adam. *Democracy and the Market.* Cambridge: Cambridge University Press, 1991.

Puzyna, Włodzimierz (member of Parliament; member, Local Government and Regional Policy Committee, Freedom Union party). Interview with author. Warsaw, July 6, 2000.

———. Interview with author. Warsaw, March 6, 2001.

Regulska, Joanna. "Building Local Democracy: The Role of Western Assistance in Poland." *Voluntas: International Journal of Voluntary and Nonprofit Organizations* 9, no. 1 (1998): 39–57.

———. "Decentralization or (Re)Centralization: Struggle for Political Power in Poland." *Environment and Planning C: Government and Policy* 15 (1997): 187–207.

———. "Local Government Reform." In *Transition to Democracy in Poland,* edited by Richard Staar. 2d edition. New York: St. Martin's Press, 1998.

———. "NGOs and their Vulnerabilities during the Time of Transition: The Case of Poland." *Voluntas: International Journal of Voluntary and Nonprofit Organizations* 10, no. 1 (1999): 61–71.

Regulska, Joanna, and Jerzy Regulski. "Local Self-Government Reform in Central and Eastern Europe." In *Democracy Building Process in Central and Eastern Europe,* edited by A. Rybczynska. Lublin, Poland: University of Maria Curie-Sklodowska University Press, 2000.

Regulski, Jerzy. "Nowy Ustrój, Nowe Szanse, Nowe Problemy." In *Podstawowe Wartości i Założenia Reformy Ustrojowej—Ustrój Samorządu Terytorialnego w Polsce (Materiały Szkoleniowe Reformy Administracji Publicznej, zeszyt 1).* Warsaw: Chancellory of the President of the Council of Ministers, 1999.

———. *Samorząd III Rzeczypospolitej—Koncepcje i Realizacja.* Warsaw: Wydawnictwo Naukowe PWN, 2000.

Remington, Thomas F., and Steven S. Smith. "Theories of Legislative Institutions and the Organization of the Russian Duma." *American Journal of Political Science* 42 (1998): 545–72.

Rivlin, A. *Reviving the American Dream.* Washington, D.C.: The Brookings Institution, 1992.

Roczek, Grzegorz. "Nauka o Powiatach." *Wspólnota* 10, no. 626 (2002): 56.

Rokita, Jan Maria (director, Institute of Public Affairs; chair, Polish Parliamentary Committee on Administration and Internal Affairs; president, Conservative Peasant Party [SKL]). Interview with author. Warsaw, March 6, 2001.

———. "Samorządowcy, Państwowcy i Psuje." *Panstwo-Rząd-Administracja (Biuletyn Programu Reformy Administracji Publicznej Instytutu Spraw Publicznych)* 7 (September, 1998): 1–4.

Rom, M., P. Peterson, and K. Scheve. "Interstate Competition and Welfare Policy." *Publius* 28, no. 3 (1998): 17–37.

Roubini, N., and J. Sachs. "Political and Economic Determinants of Budget Deficits in the Industrial Democracies." *European Economic Review* 33 (May, 1989): 903–33.

Rousseau, M., and R. Zariski. *Regionalism and Regional Devolution in Comparative Perspective.* New York: Praeger, 1987.

Schickler, Eric. *Disjointed Pluralism: Institutional Innovation and the Development of the U.S. Congress.* Princeton: Princeton University Press, 2001.

Sekuła, Mirosław (chair, Polish Parliamentary Committee on Public Finance; member, Solidarity Electoral Action; member, Silesian Voivodship [Provincial] Parliament). Interview with author. Warsaw, July 12, 2000.

Shah, Anwar. *Balance, Accountability, and Responsiveness: Lessons about Decentralization.* Policy Research Working Paper No. WPS2021. Washington, D.C.: World Bank, 1998.

Smith, B. *Decentralization: The Territorial Dimension of the State.* London: George Allen and Unwin, 1985.

Strubinska, Małgorzata. "Proteza Zamiast Ustawy." *Wspólnota* 31, no. 542 (2000): 9.

———. "Samorządowe Urzędy Pracy." *Wspólnota* 2, no. 513 (2000): 2.

Surazska, W., J. Bucek, L. Malikova, and P. Danek. "Towards Regional Government in Central Europe: Territorial Restructuring of Postcommunist Regimes." *Environment and Planning C: Government and Policy* 14 (1996): 437–62.

Szarek, Ryszard. "Powiatowe Centrum Pomocy Rodzinie." *Wspólnota* 12, no. 523 (2000): 22.

Szczerbiak, Aleks. "Interests and Values: Polish Parties and Their Electorates." *Europe-Asia Studies* 51, no. 8 (1999):1401–32.

Taras, Ray. "Democratic Centralism and Polish Local Government Reforms." *London: Public Administration* 53 (winter, 1975): 403–26.

Ter-Minassian, Teresa. "Decentralizing Government." *Finance and Development* 34, no. 3 (1997): 36–39.

Tkaczyk, Maria. "Zespoły Orzekające o Stopniu Niepełnosprawności." In *Raport z Realizacji Projektu Badawczego Zadania Społeczne Powiatu dla Ministerstwa Spraw Wewnętrznych i Administracji,* by J. Hrynkiewicz et al. Warsaw: Institute of Applied Social Sciences, University of Warsaw, 1999.

Tomaszewska, Ewa (vice chair, Polish Parliamentary Committee on Social Policy; member, Solidarity Electoral Action; member, National Commission of the Independent Self-Governing Trade Union "SOLIDARITY"). Interview with author. Warsaw, September 15, 2000.

Ulanowska, Lidia. "Domy Pomocy Społecznej." In *Raport z Realizacji Projektu Badawczego Zadania Społeczne Powiatu dla Ministerstwa Spraw Wewnętrznych i Administracji,* by J. Hrynkiewicz et al. Warsaw: Institute of Applied Social Sciences, University of Warsaw, 1999.

United Nations. *Decentralization: Conditions for Success.* New York: Department for Economic and Social Affairs, Division for Public Economics and Public Administration, United Nations, 1999.

Waldo, Dwight. *The Administrative State: A Study of the Political Theory of American Public Administration.* 2nd edition. New York: Holmes and Meier Publishers, 1984.

Watson, M. "Conclusion: A Comparative Evaluation of Planning Practice in the Liberal Democratic State." In *Planning, Politics, and Public Policy: The British, French, and Italian Experience,* edited by L. Binder et al. London: Cambridge University Press, 1975.

Wawrzynkiewicz, Danuta (advisor to the minister of finance, former head of the Department of Local Government Finances, Ministry of Finance). Interview with author. Warsaw, June 19, 2001.

Weaver, K., and B. Rockman. *Do Institutions Matter? Government Capabilities in the United States and Abroad.* Washington, D.C.: Brookings Institution, 1993.

Weber, Maria. "Nowy Rok—Stare Kłopoty." *Wspólnota* 52–53, no. 563–64 (2000): 38–39.

———. "O Nas bez Nas." *Wspólnota* 19, no. 53 (2000): 7.

Wejner, A., and J. Błędowski. "Krajowy Urząd Pracy Kontra Starostwie: Agonia Form Aktywnych." *Wspólnota* 25, no. 536 (2000): 8–9.

White, S., J. Blatt, and P. Lewis, eds. *Developments in East European Politics.* New York: Macmillan and Co., 1993.

Willis, E., C. Garman, and S. Haggard. "The Politics of Decentralization in Latin America." *Latin American Research Review* 34, no. 1 (1999): 7–56.

Wollman, Hellmut. "Institution Building and Decentralization in Formerly Socialist Countries: The Cases of Poland, Hungary, and East Germany." *Environment and Planning C: Government and Policy* 15 (1997): 463–80.

World Bank. *Corruption in Poland: Review of Priority Areas and Proposals for Action.* Warsaw: World Bank (Poland), 1999.

———. *The Online Sourcebook on Decentralization and Local Government.* From www.ciesin.org/decentralization/SB., 2001.

Wygnański, J. J. " Elementy Budowania i Uczęstnictwa w Programach Wspólpracy Organizacji Pozarządowych z Administracją Publiczną." *Roczniak* 4 (1998): 15–34.

Yin, Robert. *Case Study Research: Design and Methods.* Thousand Oaks, Calif.: Sage Publications, 1994.

Zaucha, J. "Regional and Local Development in Poland." In *Decentralization and Transition in the Visegrad,* edited by E. Kirchner. New York: St. Martin's Press, 1999.

Związek Powiatów Polskich (Association of Polish Counties). *Monitorowanie Działalności Powiatów Polskich—Raport 1.* Nowy Sącz: Związek Powiatów Polskich, 1999.

Index

Tables and maps are indicated with *italic* type.

ISBN 1-58544-417-0

53900

9 781585 444175